The Psychology of Supremacy

The Psychology of Supremacy brings a developmental, philosophical and psychological lens to understanding the systems embedded within the socially constructed aspects of our intersectional identities.

Offering a philosophical understanding of supremacy and its meaning within counselling and psychotherapy, the book examines just how and why supremacy exists, some of the psychology behind supremacy, and how it impacts clients, training, and practice. Chapters offer means and ways of observing and challenging systems of supremacy as they may appear within counselling and psychotherapy relationships. Featured psychotherapeutic case studies detail stories from participants who have endured the painful experience of being involved in the power structures of supremacy.

A must read for psychotherapists and counsellors, this book will also appeal to psychologists, social workers, qualitative and quantitative researchers, and anyone else interested in further deepening their understanding of supremacy, privilege, and otherness.

Dr Dwight Turner, is an activist, a writer and public speaker on issues of race, difference and intersectionality in counselling and psychotherapy. He is a Course Leader in Humanistic Counselling at the University of Brighton.

The Psychology of Supremacy

Imperium

Dwight Turner

Routledge
Taylor & Francis Group

LONDON AND NEW YORK

Cover image: © Getty Images

First published 2024
by Routledge
4 Park Square, Milton Park, Abingdon, Oxon OX14 4RN

and by Routledge
605 Third Avenue, New York, NY 10158

Routledge is an imprint of the Taylor & Francis Group, an informa business

British Library Cataloguing-in-Publication Data
A catalogue record for this book is available from the British Library

Library of Congress Cataloguing-in-Publication Data
Names: Turner, Dwight, author.
Title: The psychology of supremacy : imperium / Dwight Turner.
Description: Abingdon, Oxon ; New York, NY : Routledge, 2024. |
Identifiers: LCCN 2023009860 (print) | LCCN 2023009861 (ebook) |
ISBN 9781032321783 (hardback) | ISBN 9781032321776 (paperback) |
ISBN 9781003313229 (ebook)
Subjects: LCSH: Racism in psychology. | Psychotherapy--Moral and ethicala aspects. | Discrimination--Psychological aspects.
Classification: LCC BF76.45 .T87 2024 (print) | LCC BF76.45 (ebook) |
DDC 155.8/2--dc23/eng/20230501
LC record available at https://lccn.loc.gov/2023009860
LC ebook record available at https://lccn.loc.gov/2023009861

ISBN: 978-1-032-32178-3 (hbk)
ISBN: 978-1-032-32177-6 (pbk)
ISBN: 978-1-003-31322-9 (ebk)

DOI: 10.4324/9781003313229

Typeset in Times New Roman
by MPS Limited, Dehradun

Contents

List of Figures   vii
Acknowledgements   viii

1   Introduction   1

Why Is It Important to Talk about Supremacy? 2
Psychotherapy and Supremacy 5
Methodological Underpinnings 7
Intersectionality and the Psychology of Supremacy 9
Summary 12

2   Imperium   15

Pillars of Supremacy 15
  Patriarchy 17
  White Supremacy 22
  Capitalism 26
Intersections of Supremacy 33
Exploring Conscious and Unconscious Supremacy 35
  Conscious Supremacy 35
  Unconscious Supremacy 46
Summary 53

3   The Psychology of Supremacy   61

The Supremacy Complex 70
Symbols of Supremacy 74
Summary 85

4 The Philosophy of Supremacy   89

The Politics of Supremacy 90
The Superiority Drive 92
The Philosophy of Supremacy 94
From Supremacy to Morality 100
    The Supremacy Defence 100
The Symbolism of Supremacy 103
Supremacy and Creativity: The Sand Tray Exercise 103
    Studying Brodie's Sand Tray 106
    Studying Dwight's Sand Tray 110
Summary 111

5 Activism and Supremacy   115

Psychotherapy as Activism 117
The Psychopathology of the Activist 122
    The Trauma Driven Activist 122
    The Morally Driven Activist 126
The Archetype of the Activist 129
Decolonising the Psyche through Dreams 132
Summary 136

6 The Climate and Supremacy   141

The Psychological Selfishness of Supremacy 143
The Climate as the Other 145
Final Words 146

Index   *149*

Figures

2.1	Conscious and Unconscious Supremacy	38
3.1	The Psychological Creation of the Other	64
3.2	How Supremacy Maintains Itself	68
3.3	Dianna's Sand Tray	76
3.4	Elsa's Sand Tray	78
3.5	Dwight's Sand Tray	82
4.1	The Supremacy Defence	100
4.2	Brodie's Sand Tray	107
5.1	The Psychology of Activism	122

Acknowledgements

I would like to extend my thanks to all at Routledge for their bravery and support as I write these books. Continued thanks to all at the University of Brighton, including Dr Niki Khan, my mentor who nudged me onto this path in the first place, and my continued thanks to all in the School of Humanities and Social Sciences as well. To my friends, Dorothy Farr, Melissa Nash, Katy Smith and Vanessa Treacey, who have advised, bollocked, held and loved me, as I walked this strange path of bringing this tome to life. Thank you for constantly being there.

Finally, my eternal thanks to my brother, Mark. We have had our differences, and we have had time apart, but my love for you, my brother, has never wavered. Onwards and upwards, this one is for you.

Chapter 1

Introduction

When I was 11 years of age, my parents sent me to a fee-paying school in London. Out of a cohort of some 150 children, I was one of only two black kids in the year. This therefore meant that I regularly endured experiences of racism, marginalisation, bullying; things that I had not experienced in my primary school, which was a lot smaller and where I was very much looked after by the teachers and the headmaster and headmistress.

My experiences at secondary school culminated in one interesting and slightly disturbing experience. When I was about 14 years of age, a group of boys in my form, four or five of them, were picking on me, taunting me and making the same racist chants that I had endured those previous three years. This was a difficult time in my life, and none of the teachers ever worked with me to stamp out the abuse that I endured regularly. During this particular altercation, for the first time, and probably the last time, I lost my cool, lashed out and pushed a boy over. The boy struck his head on the skirting board of the room, cracking his head open. Everything stopped. At that moment, a couple of other boys came in and they picked this young man up and took him off to see the nurse.

As was inevitable, we were both hauled into the headmaster's office later on that day. Whilst the other boy had a couple of stitches, I was just mortally embarrassed at having lost my cool. We were both given the cane; he got one lash for being part of the group of kids who were bullying me, and I got two, because I was the one who had lost his cool and pushed him over.

I tell this story not so much for vindication of my own experience making this some sort of racialised bloodletting, but to give you an idea of the different intersecting layers of supremacy that were involved in this whole scenario. My parents had chosen to send me to a private feepaying school in Central London, whereas many of their peers, and of my cousins, were unable to afford much more than sending their kids to the local comprehensive. There was a predominance of whiteness in the school and the marginalisation of those who were deemed as other, be they Asian or black, like myself and the other boy of colour. There is also the capitalist element, where this was an incredibly expensive school, so much so that my parents, who were both working class

DOI: 10.4324/9781003313229-1

immigrants from the Caribbean, literally worked day and night in order to send me to a school matching me alongside the children of parents who were anything from diplomats to accountants to those on large salaries in the City of London.

Supremacy, the main theme for this book, is etched all the way through this story in ways that we will explore as I expand on this further on. It is a facet of Western culture that has existed since the days of the ancient Greeks. It is so complex and nuanced and so embedded, that when we raise ideas of just what supremacy is, we are often left with a sense that we are talking about something alien, something foreign, something that cannot possible be so true because it sounds so ugly, so grotesque, so false.

The aim of this book though is not to vilify supremacy, but instead to unpack the intersections of supremacy, be they patriarchy, white supremacy and capitalism. This book looks to explore some of the history around these three intersections of supremacy, before considering some of the psychological narratives that underpin their continued existence, their continued vibrancy, their continued life. Then finally we will then consider how, as per any experience, we inevitably will have internalised supremacy and be playing these experiences out, either in our day-to-day lives or as witnesses to this with our clients and our supervisees and on our courses.

I need to make this very clear from the start of this book there will not be a single person reading this text who would not have internalised the white supremacist, capitalist, patriarchy in some way. It could well be that we fight for the rights of others based upon class difference for example, whilst also ordering the latest book, record, item online from Amazon. It may well be that we claim to believe in equality, whilst also often unconsciously marginalising and oppressing other groups around us. It may well be that we believe that all races are equal, but that we then whitesplain racism to those who have most endured it.

The internalised supremacist is a massive aspect of who we all are. As part of our superego, it helps us to form our identity, it builds us up and it creates images, examples of who we believe we happen to be in relation to others.

Why Is It Important to Talk about Supremacy?

At the time of writing, there are at present in London approximately 25 traditional Gentleman's Clubs. Of these 25, many of these have existed for between 150 and 170 years. A good number of these were established during the early period of capitalism here in the United Kingdom and the general ethos of such clubs is that they were places exclusively designed for men, normally white upper-class men to go, sit, eat, do business, and discuss the politics of the day with their peers and such. Conversely, these environments were also designed to exclude; women were often not allowed to attend, the working classes were often marginalised (or were placed in a role of service within such a club) and anyone of any other type of difference, be it racial or cultural, was often denied membership of such a club. In fact, for all of those marginalised groups that I have just mentioned, the best that they could ever probably afford was to become a member of staff serving those above them as they did their daily, weekly, and monthly business.

The reason for telling this sort of story is that the fact that these clubs still exist shows the institutional nature of exclusion within English culture. This is so apparent, that there are a number, at the time of writing, of court cases going through the whereby individuals, more often than not, have sought fit to challenge the prejudicial nature of such clubs in the modern era. Their argument being that membership should not just be offered to those who are male and are of the upper or middle classes but should also be afforded to women and other groups, people who perhaps can afford the high fees to join such a club (Bendell, 2020).

This shows how systemic, and also in this case institutional, prejudice and marginalisation actually are, and just how its existence has always relied upon the exclusion of the other. This is an important factor to recognise. The second thing to be able to explore here is this; often times I hear stories whereby leaders of organisations come out and suggest that they know of nobody who is prejudice, sexist, homophobic, or racist within their organisation and yet these very same issues of racism, homophobia, or sexism have been raised against said organisation. This is an important factor in understanding that what has been discussed, the systemic versus the individual are just that, two very separate things.

Private members clubs were established with a certain ethos and set of characteristics and rules that worked to marginalise; and yet it is also quite reasonable to assume that those individuals who work for said institution may well not be sexist, homophobic, racist, ableist, ageist, or any other form of -obia or -ism. The problem with this dichotomy is that whilst those individuals are employed by such an organisation, their normal, and in some cases moral, response to systems of injustice has to be put to one side in order to facilitate the everyday ongoings of said organisation. So, the individual, who will inevitably be a part of said organisation, is both racist, sexist, homophobic, etc. and at the same time they are not. Their acceptance of this dichotomy, of what Lacan might say is a psychological split within their own psyche, emerges through a process of self-othering that leaves them in collusion with the organisation (Lacan, 2003). The price therefore to pay for being a member of an organisation such as this is the othering of one's own moral standpoint around systems of injustice (D. D. L. Turner, 2021).

Whilst I am raising this important factor here, it also recognises this is something that we all do in order to belong to any organisation or system or group, because we all buy into its ethos. This is where the idea of *The Psychology of Supremacy* then takes a hold because ultimately, we all have a vested interest in belonging and yet the groups that we choose to belong to, the companies that hire us, the families we belong within, the culture, the religion. All of these will have a way of being which will run counter to, for some of us, the inherent underlying moral standpoints that we may or may not tap into. That is not to say though, that there will not be those people who will fully buy into the organisational ethos, maybe because it suits them or maybe because it is just an easier path to follow. There will always be people who will do this. What it is to say is that for those who want to challenge the system, the systemic oppressions, who want to decolonise the curriculum, who want to de-institutionalise racism and sexism from major organisations such as the police or the military.

In 2021, Routledge published the book *Intersections of Privilege and Otherness in Counselling and Psychotherapy #Mockingbird* (D. D. L. Turner, 2021). This well received book dealt a lot with issues of privilege and otherness in counselling and psychotherapy. What this book did not do is actually look at how supremacy exists, instead only acknowledging that this is formed out of privilege, and that it is more of a destructive influence in the psychotherapy dyad than privilege is when considered and held appropriately. For example, within psychotherapy whilst there have been considerations of difference and diversity, what we have recently seen, especially here in the United Kingdom, is a political shift away from the politics of equality and the re-emergence of white supremacy. For example, in 2021 the Commission for Racial Equality produced a report denying the existence of institutional racism within the United Kingdom (Commission on Race and Ethnic Disparities, 2021). The Tory Government of the time posted that the United Kingdom was at the forefront in the fight for equal rights for different races within this country. They said that the actual issue is more of a socioeconomic one than ever was around race.

At this same time, post the murder of George Floyd, which I will discuss further on in this chapter, English footballers were regularly taking the knee during the football Euros which were held across the continent during June of said year. That these protests were booed by their own fans and often criticised by their own Government, shows how much in conflict the ideas of the commissioned report were, the Seeley report, was in relation to the lived experience of persons of colour within this country (Merrick & White, 2021).

Also, during this period, in the early part of 2021, Sarah Everard, a 33-year-old British woman who lived in London, was sadly murdered by a policeman whilst on her way home from a night out. The vigils that were held in her honour were as much to protest against male violence as they were about the death of one individual. Yet, in a judgement from such a patriarchal organisation as the police, these vigils were strangely deemed outside the law on many occasions, a decision that seemed to fuel the divisions between the different genders within this country (Morton, 2021).

Also during 2021, the Intergovernmental Panel for Climate Change produced a report detailing the full impact of climate change upon the planet

(IPCC, 2021). A damning report, this emphasised that in many ways we have crossed a number of Rubicon's which mean that we are beyond certain points of no return. The emphasis of this report was also to say that there were numerous groups, numerous poorer nations around the globe that were suffering and struggling to cope with the growing demands of the climate crisis. That this report was published at the same time as some of the richest men on the planet were flying into space is testimony to how driven those who believe in capitalist supremacy are to maintaining their position over the 'third world' other and the working classes in their own nations (Unknown, 2021; Various, 2021a).

All of these simple examples of supremacy's oppression of otherness would have been felt by our clients within the psychotherapy room. Be they women who are reminded that they feel unsafe in male environments, to persons of colour, of difference, who knew what was going to happen as soon as three English footballers of colour missed penalties in the finals of the European Football Championships (Besley, 2021; Various, 2021b); to those whose social economic status has been very much impacted by the rise of capitalist ideals. Ultimately, we will all have encountered clients for whom the fight to survive supremacy's iron grip is a day-to-day, week-to-week, month-to-month struggle.

Psychotherapy and Supremacy

When George Floyd was murdered on 25 May 2020, numerous companies across the country, across the world in fact, moved hell and high water to actually make a change in the face of what they finally recognise was the systemic oppression of persons of colour. My own experience of witnessing George Floyd's murder actually involved me trying to shy away from the full psychological traumatic impact of seeing yet another man of colour murdered on the streets of a global northern town. A colleague mere days after his death asked me to write a blog about what it is to be a man of colour in this era, and my initial response to said request was to actually say no. It was too much for me to take on, it was too close to home. It was frankly too painful a thing for me to talk to or talk about.

That night, something woke me up at 5:00 am. When I woke up, I made the fatal mistake of checking my Twitter feed. Witnessing the numerous protests, riots, symbolic gestures of solidarity, not just in America but across the world, against the systemic oppression of persons of colour, had me both moved and angry. I got up that night and I sat down in front of my computer and I wrote 2,500 words into a blog entitled Black Steel in the Hour of Chaos (D. D. Turner, 2020). This was the blog that I sent to the friend who had asked me originally. She published it and together we watched it go viral. Prominent psychotherapists, many of whom are well known in this field in the United Kingdom and in the United States, re-tweeted this blog. Organisations contacted me on the back of my expression of pain and sadness, asking me to take part in panel discussions and conferences where explorations of race, racism, white supremacy, white fragility would take place. Finally, the world of psychotherapy had decided to take issues of race and difference seriously.

Psychotherapy has long been reluctant to engage with the political sphere. It has rejected calls on numerous occasions to offer its own insights, its own perspectives on how to challenge some of the political narratives of our times. This contrasts with numerous others who rejected this call to politics as it could have led to their own positions of privilege and supremacy being challenged. Whereas writers such as Frosh (2003, 2008), Samuels (1998, 2001), and others have tried to make their cases for how the psychotherapeutic community might offer not only an understanding of the psychological impact of political decisions but also a roadmap as to how psychotherapy might influence the political sphere. The closest perhaps we have ever gotten to exploring the systemic violence that our clients walk with on a day-to-day basis will be through an exploration of the power dynamics which radiate within our psychotherapy rooms (Proctor, 2010; Stevens, 2021). This can either be used for the benefit of our clients to empower them so they can grasp the greater responsibility in their world, or in the worst cases have led to the abuses of said power from therapist to client, where on numerous occasions practitioners have been struck off or have been forced to leave the trade.

Simultaneously, this is a profession which sends nearly all of its trainees out to work in placements within charities, often with clients who are not only from deprived cultural backgrounds. They will often encounter clients whose social economic struggles are a core part of their experience. What this can culminate in is that clients often are told to explore the blocks to their achieving more, that they just need to 'work a bit harder', 'to pull their bootstraps up', that actually they could achieve as much as anybody else by a therapist of privilege who then gets into their nice fancy car and drives off to a country home. I can only imagine how not just infuriating this must be for working class clients and students alike, but also how incredibly patronising this neglect of the social economic reality of said client group must be.

Offering another perspective, there was the time I heard a male lecturer tell a female student that she needed to cover up, lest her cleavage attract attention from her clients. It was an issue which left the student feeling ashamed, but also left persons like myself furious at the treatment of a woman by a patriarch who was again unaware of his own power, privilege, and supremacy in said interaction.

These are just a couple of the numerous examples of how superiority and supremacy play a dominant role in the interactions as much in the wider culture as they are within psychotherapy. Psychotherapy therefore has a duty to look at just how systemic oppression impacts upon the therapeutic alliance and to neglect, nay to ignore and reject this responsibility, is nothing short than the same cultural dereliction of duty that permeates the current political landscape where we witness the constant denial of systemic oppression of any and all groups of others.

To take this a stage further, most of our private organisations are set up within a capitalist system whereby as well as needing to make money and function, the fact that the fees are so high in many cases, therefore excludes huge swathes of the potential counselling and psychotherapy student landscape from even taking on this difficult task of becoming a practitioner. Capitalism, when tied to psychotherapy, then reinforces huge levels of inequality both within the profession and without the profession where practitioners are working with clients who are very different to themselves. In fact, I would go even further and say capitalism needs inequalities for it to actually exist; it is not interested in equity. Therefore, psychotherapy and counselling courses are unequal because of the system of capitalism they are embedded within, and if psychotherapy is a mirror for wider society, then it must also be assumed that these inequalities will sit within our therapeutic spaces accordingly.

So, returning to my earlier point, even the forefathers within psychotherapy have had a lot to say about the political and the systemic oppressions of their times. Wilhelm Reich (1970) wrote about the rise of Nazism and its impact upon society. Whereas Sigmund Freud (1930) himself, who many seem to interestingly consider apolitical, wrote as much about the rise of fascism prior to his own need to leave the country as any of the other early psychodynamic therapists. Ours is a profession, which has fallen under the whispered words of the hypnotist that is supremacy, so much so that we have given up our voice in the constant cultural struggle that involves not only being seen but being free as well. This book is therefore as much an attempt to re-ignite the spark of the fire that will challenge said systemic oppression within psychotherapy as it is to provide an avenue for the voices of those who feel not only dispossessed of language and opinion, but also oppressed by their own circumstances and internalised oppressor.

Methodological Underpinnings

It was Hegel (1976) who said that culture does not move in a straight line in its progression towards completion. His view being that culture meanders like a river, it starts at its source, it rolls downhill, it backs up on itself as it has to negotiate different obstacles along the way. The cultural climate that we are living within mirrors this in that this is a culture whereby we have seen numerous progressions in women's rights, in the right for global change for workers' rights, in the battle for climate change to ensure the survival of our human race with regard to racism and civil rights, homophobia and the right to self-identify within the LBTQ community (Andrews & Palmer, 2013; Butler, 1999; Davies & Neal, 2000).

Yet, as with any sort of cultural movement, there have been times whereby culture has felt like it has reverted back upon itself. For example, in the reversion of the movement towards ending conversion therapy by the British Government, or in the repealing of certain acts that were deemed to create a more equal playing field for persons of colour in both the United Kingdom and the United States (Young, 2018). These moments in political history are perhaps symptomatic of culture's inability to move straight ahead with itself and the very human resistance to move away from a process of supremacy to one of relational equity and equanimity.

The impact of this upon culture is therefore felt within our psychotherapy and counselling spaces. From those clients who will have been impacted by the increase in National Insurance contributions at the end of a pandemic, to those same groups of immigrants and workers and working classes who would have been impacted disproportionately by the impact of COVID and lockdowns upon their lives and their lifestyles (Ahrens et al., 2021; Jacques-Avinõ et al., 2020; Unknown, 2020). The political, as always, is a constant factor in the lives of those who are seen as being less advantaged.

My work though takes a phenomenological approach to understanding these cultural experiences. Borrowing from the work of Merleau-Ponty (1962), phenomenology is the collective experience of phenomena together with how that said phenomena impacts upon ourselves, our bodily selves even. This book is therefore derived from my doctoral work and also from my own client material and experiences, whereby I interview 25 people about their own experience of being an outsider, returning to some of that material has therefore gleaned a deeper understanding of how supremacy works within the psyche.

To get to this, it was essential though to do a lot of body work with my participants. Bodywork being the route towards the unconscious and the internalised felt embodied experience of supremacy as we walk through it on a day-to-day, week-to-week, year-to-year basis (Lowen, 2013). Alongside this, it was also felt essential for me to use creative work, in this case sand play work. Derived by Jungian analysts, many years ago, including Dora Kalff (1991), this way of working involves the externalisation or internalised objects given that every experience that we ever have will be internalised.

Often when we talk about internalisation though, from a more psycho-dynamic perspective this involves the internalised object being a positive from one's parents, our mother, our primary care givers whoever it might be, and the positive influence they have had upon us (Ogden, 2004). The difficulty with this approach is that it starts to marginalise the more difficult experiences of internalisation that we all go through; the abusive partner, the difficult teacher at school, the horrible manager are all symptoms of our internalised world and will all have become symbols of said world. So, using creative techniques are therefore an incredibly important way of externalising that.

Alongside this, I will be using dream work to show how the internalised supremacist sits quite deep in one's psyche and even offering a solution as to what this might be when it has been worked with. Touching on trauma work as well as an essential part of my work here, with the trauma of the process of othering being a central tenet to the internalisation process of the cultural gender, racial, capitalist supremacist and how, without exploring this aspect of ourselves, we are therefore left with a part within us that will always play itself out and look for others to marginalise so to speak (Johnson, 1986; Stein, 2005).

Intersectionality and the Psychology of Supremacy

This book will also marry together intersectionality and phenomenology. In a way, the work of Patricia Hill Collins (2019) is important here in that she clearly understood that the intersections of capitalism, patriarchy, and white supremacy were core aspects in understanding experiences of difference and otherness and that exploring just one of these alone would be ineffectual as it would fail to unpack all the experience of difference and otherness that we encounter every day. What this also means though is that any real understanding of the collective experience of oppression must therefore be taken through a phenomenological lens. This view, raised by myself, recognises that oppression is a phenomenological experience for anyone, so to attempt to express what happens in its singular form is therefore to miss the more nuanced aspects of this that are experienced by other across the world. This is why there is so much confusion around just what racism, sexism, and homophobia actually are. This is why any real understanding of that has to be explored through a collective lens, not a singular one.

This exploration will therefore be conducted by recognising that when we speak of systemic oppression, what we are actually speaking off is the triumvirate of white supremacy, patriarchy, and capitalism. This is important to recognise as often any sort of attempt to create equality in just one of these areas often leaves the other two areas untouched and therefore free to act from their own position. For example, ideas of instituting equal numbers of women on boards of major companies, whilst commendable do not actually look at systemic levels of oppression that perhaps persons of colour endure in those environments or that those who are from working class backgrounds may encounter in trying to achieve the same levels of success as their higher-class colleagues. A perfect example of this is the constant separating out of gender pay gaps, say for example at the BBC (2019) where we often seen the gender pay gap as something which is based around the white middle classes. Whereas issues around race within the BBC are often missed or are separated off into a separate categorisation.

Whilst my previous book will have concentrated a fair amount more on the racialised aspects of difference and otherness, this one will take a different tack. In looking a lot more at capitalism, there is more space here to look at how class plays a massive role in oppressions and otherness, and also at how patriarchy oppresses not just women but also creates and reinforces systems of toxic masculinity for men as well. This does not mean that this issues around race, difference and homophobia will not be considered in this book, but it does mean that this argument will be expanded considerably as we look to explore just what is supremacy and how it actually works.

The following chapters will therefore look at just how supremacy is defined through an intersectional lens, looking at capitalism, patriarchy, and white supremacy, together with how they impact on our conscious world through their structures, through the political narratives that underpin them, through how we live with them on a day-to-day basis.

There will also be a consideration of the origins of patriarchy, the origins of capitalism and how white supremacy is a more recent construct built out of the pair of these. This chapter will consider the cultural racial and gender structures which help to maintain these pillars of systemic oppression as being core to the Western cultural landscape.

We will also look at how these historical beginnings have led to constant evolution within these systems, so that as Foucault (Foucault & Miskowiec, 2012) suggests in his writings, any attempt to undermine or disrupt them is not so much doomed to failure but will take generations. This assessment is because these are systems which have existed for, in some cases, hundreds of years and in others literally thousands. For example, I recently saw a poster from one of the vigils for Sarah Everard whereby the poster actually stated something along the lines of 'Why am I still protesting this shit?' Now, whilst well-meaning and whilst the statement itself, speaks of the tiresome fighting for equality that women have to go through culminating presently with the #MeToo movement, what it also recognises is how deeply entrenched patriarchal supremacy over women actually is and how detrimental it is to the psyche of those on the receiving end. This is important as this chapter will continue to state, that instead of perhaps taking a generation to unpick, unpack and dismantle systems of patriarchy, white supremacy or capitalism, that this may take generations plural. Any struggle for equality or equity has to bear this in mind; there is a longer-term cultural chess game to be played here if one is to win.

Within this tome, we will also take a deeper exploration into the psychological underpinning of systems of supremacy. This will involve exploring the developmental stages that we go through in forming a sense of sense of self and how supremacy therefore becomes a natural facet in the sense of building an ego over its shadow other. There will also be an exploration of the psychological, existential, psychodynamic, and spiritual meaning of supremacy through a psychotherapeutic lens together with just how the combination of these systems of psychological oppression reinforce a sense of outsideness and a feeling of less than.

There will also be an exploration of trauma and how trauma then creates and reinforces the internalised supremacist. This is followed by an exploration of just how and when it plays out in later life, and that when we marginalise the other, and take a superior stance over them what we are doing is talking from within, or from the traumatic experiences of childhood or even adulthood from our inner wounded self which is holding something painful and difficult from the past.

We again will return to notions of internalisation here whilst also exploring how the nature of woundedness and trauma has become incredibly normalised within our culture, but we are led by systems of supremacy is because they are driven by traumatised adults much of the time. It is important therefore to explore the internalised supremacist. I will touch on the more nuanced nature of day-to-day experiences of supremacy, including mansplaining, subtle put-downs, microaggressions, and how these then reinforce the sense that one who is better than or superior to the other, before using creativity to unpack how these experiences may actually display themselves in the therapeutic space. As stated, much of this material will be presented creatively through the lens of sand play work. This gentle means of working with the unconscious has been used here because when our clients come to see us, more often than not it is the negative or the more challenging internalised aspects of our care givers, our environment or the cultural, racial or gendered narratives that have been passed on to us that are causing us pain and restricting us in our growth and our movement towards individuation (Taylor, 2009; B. A. Turner, 2005). So, if we are living in a system of oppression, then it makes perfect sense that at some point that aspect of our experience of our culture etc. will have become inter-nalised and will have become an object within our unconscious self. Sand play work is therefore an essential and an incredibly powerful way to externalise these internalised objects. Moving beyond the mind, this externalisation of internalised objects allows practitioners, theorists, and psychotherapists to see and to help our clients witness the darker material they have held within them. This material will often have been projected on to others, partners, and organisations. It is therefore for our participants and our clients to see this in a non-intrusive and yet strongly powerful way, is a means for them to start to recognise, to own and to re-integrate or re-format that which has become offensive, destructive and in many cases abusive of the other.

I will also be including dream work to help explore how the internalised experience of supremacy then plays itself out within the dreamscape to such a deep extent that this symbol is always contained within our dreams. According to Jung (D. Turner, 2016), our dreams often contain aspects of a repressed sense of self within this dream landscape whatever we have denied of our own experience will appear in some format. To give you a lived ex-ample from my own sort of dreamscape, there was a day back in 2020 when I attended a meeting to discuss issues around difference and otherness. During said meeting, a colleague decided to actually express his opinion that what I was talking about was not based around issues of race and difference but was located within the realm of Attachment Theory (Bowlby, 1973, 1988). Given the years or experience that I have had, and the numerous papers that I have written, and the experience of Klansplaining that I endure, that particular night I then had the following dream:

> The dream involved my walking out of Barons Court tube station, turning left and walking down the hill towards the Talgarth Road. As I walked down the hill, on the top of a wall there is a white man with a machine gun. He has Nazi insignia on his face and is wearing combat outfit. He starts to open fire on myself and the crowd around us, injuring or killing people about myself. Together with a group of black and white men, we all tackle this man, take him to the ground and pummel him unconscious. In this dream, I then get up and I look back to see that my girlfriend, a black woman has fallen to the ground behind me. She has been shot. I rush over to her and try to comfort her as she gives me a magazine with cars and trucks within it. She dies in my arms. I wake up screaming and in tears.

This dream is just one example of the deeper psychological impact of internalised supremacy and spoke to myself and to my own therapist about just how painful it was to have my own work undermined by a said colleague. It also revealed to myself just how much of me was the Nazi in the dream. As Carl Jung (1964) states, each character within a dreamscape is actually a part of the dreamer themselves. So, as well as being the black woman who dies, the part of my racial culture that dies a death in my own arms, I have also had activated within myself the internalised supremacist that takes up arms and self-mutilates my own psyche. Understanding the power of this dream is essential here. When considering the experiences of our clients when they walk through patriarchal environments as women, when they endure the jibes of the middle classes at school when they come from a working-class background, the internalised impact should not be underestimated.

The conclusion will tie all these ideas together, together with a restatement of how we as practitioners can work with this material to help ourselves and our clients and in our training courses as well.

Summary

This book aims to be the first of its kind to open up a deeper exploration of how the intersections of white supremacy, patriarchy, and capitalism impact on the lives of our clients and of ourselves as counselling and psychotherapy practitioners. Whilst this book will include a good deal of theory and philosophical and political material, there will also be a good number of anonymised case presentations designed to elucidate the lived experiences of all our clients.

To therefore begin this exploration, the next chapter will consider the historical backdrop to patriarchy, white supremacy and capitalism.

References

Ahrens, K. F., Neumann, R. J., Kollmann, B., Plichta, M. M., Lieb, K., Tüscher, O., & Reif, A. (2021). Differential impact of COVID-related lockdown on mental health in Germany. *World Psychiatry*, *20*(1), 140–141. 10.1002/wps.20830

Andrews, K., & Palmer, L. (2013). Why Black Studies matters. *Discover Society*, *2*, 1–4.

BBC. (2019). Gender pay gap. In *BBC Gender Pay Gap*. https://iba.org/datafiles/publicacoes/relatorios/iba-relatorioanual2019.pdf

Bendell, E. (2020). Businesswoman launches legal action against the Garrick Club. Guardian Online. https://www.theguardian.com/world/2020/sep/08/businesswoman-launches-legal-action-against-the-garrick-club

Besley, J. (2021). Euro 2020: FA condemns racist abuse of England players after shootout defeat. Independent Online. https://www.independent.co.uk/sport/football/saka-sancho-rashford-racism-england-euros-b1882325.html

Bowlby, J. (1973). *Separation*. Pimlico.

Bowlby, J. (1988). *A Secure Base: Parent-Child Attachment and Healthy Human Development*. Basic Books. 10.1097/00005053-199001000-00017

Butler, J. (1999). *Gender Trouble*. Routledge.

Collins, P. H. (2019). *Intersectionality as Critical Social Theory*. Duke University Press.

Commission on Race and Ethnic Disparities. (2021). *Commission on Race and Ethnic Disparities: The Report* (Issue March). https://assets.publishing.service.gov.uk/government/uploads/system/uploads/attachment_data/file/974507/20210331_-_CRED_Report_-_FINAL_-_Web_Accessible.pdf

Davies, D., & Neal, C. (2000). *Therapeutic Perspectives on Working with Lesbian, Gay and Bisexual Clients*. Open University Press.

Foucault, M., & Miskowiec, J. (2012). Texts/contexts of other spaces. *Diacritics*, *16*(1), 22–27.

Freud, S. (1930). *Civilisation and Its Discontents*. Penguin Limited.

Frosh, S., & Baraitser, L. (2003). Thinking, recognition, and otherness. *Psychoanalytic Review*, *90*(6), 771–789. http://www.ncbi.nlm.nih.gov/pubmed/15150846

Frosh, S., & Baraitser, L. (2008). Marginalia. *Qualitative Research in Psychology*, *5*(1), 68–77. 10.1080/14780880701863591

Hegel, G. (1976). *Phenomenology of Spirit*. Oxford University Press.

IPCC. (2021). IPCC press release AR6. *Climate Change 2013 – The Physical Science Basis, August 2021*, 1–6.

Jacques-Avinõ, C., López-Jiménez, T., Medina-Perucha, L., De Bont, J., Gonçalves, A. Q., Duarte-Salles, T., & Berenguera, A. (2020). Gender-based approach on the social impact and mental health in Spain during COVID-19 lockdown: A cross-sectional study. *BMJ Open*, *10*(11), 1–10. 10.1136/bmjopen-2020-044617

Johnson, R. A. (1986). *Inner Work: Using Dreams and Active Imagination for Personal Growth*. Harper San Francisco.

Jung, C. G. (1964). *Man and His Symbols*. Picador.

Kalff, D. M. (1991). Introduction to Sandplay Therapy. *Journal of Sandplay Therapy*, *1*(1), 1–4.

Lacan, J. (2003). *The Cambridge Companion to Lacan* (J.-M. Rabate (ed.)). Cambridge University Press. 10.1017/CCOL0521807441

Lowen, A. (2013). *The Language of the Body*. The Alexander Lowen Foundation.

Merleau-Ponty, M. (1962). *The Phenomenology of Perception*. Routledge.

Merrick, R., & White, N. (2021). *United Nations experts condemn 'shocking' race report and call for Commission to be scrapped.* Independent Online. https://www. independent.co.uk/news/uk/politics/race-report-un-boris-johnson-commission-b1833671.html

Morton, B. (2021). *Sarah Everard: How Wayne Couzens planned her murder.* BBC News Online. https://www.bbc.co.uk/news/uk-58746108

Ogden, T. H. (2004). On holding and containing, being and dreaming. *The International Journal of Psycho-Analysis, 85*(Pt 6), 1349–1364. http://www.ncbi.nlm. nih.gov/pubmed/15801512

Proctor, G. (2010). Boundaries or mutuality in therapy: is mutuality really possible or is therapy doomed from the start? *Psychotherapy and Politics International, 8*(1), 44–58. 10.1002/ppi

Reich, W. (1970). *The Mass Psychology of Facism* (3rd ed.). Soverign Press.

Samuels, A. (1998). 'And if not now, when?': spirituality, psychotherapy, politics. *Psychodynamic Counselling, 4*(3), 349–365. 10.1080/13533339808402515

Samuels, A. (2001). The secret life of politics. In *Politics on the Couch: Citizenship and the Internal Life* (pp. 1–14). Routledge.

Stein, M. (2005). Individuation: Inner Work. *Journal of Jungian Theory and Practice, 7*(2), 1–13.

Stevens, E. (2021). National Counsellors' Day Conference – Saturday 19th June 2021 – Theme: Intersectionality, discrimination and social justice: a call for true equality in Counselling and Psychotherapy. In CTUK (Ed.), *Facing the Shadow of Harm in Therapy.* (p. 1). https://www.nationalcounsellorsday.co.uk/erin-stevens/

Taylor, E. R. (2009). Sandtray and solution-focused therapy. *International Journal of Play Therapy, 18*(1), 56–68. 10.1037/a0014441

Turner, B. A. (2005). *The Handbook of Sandplay Therapy.* Tenemos Press.

Turner, D. (2016). Born Again: An alchemical exploration of the dreams of the Other. *IASD, 45,* 1–8.

Turner, D. D. (2020). *Black Steel in the Hour of Chaos.* BME Voices. https://www. bmevoices.co.uk/black-steel-in-the-hour-of-chaos/

Turner, D. D. L. (2021). *Intersections of Privilege and Otherness in Counselling and Psychotherapy* (1st ed.). Routledge.

Unknown (2020). BAME people are hit hardest by depression during lockdown. *The Daily Telegraph,* July, 2020–2021. https://search.proquest.com/docview/ 2419580438?accountid=9727

Unknown (2021). *Greta Thunberg: 'COP26 even watered down the blah, blah, blah'.* BBC News Online. https://www.bbc.co.uk/news/av/uk-scotland-59298344

Various (2021a). *Amazon's Jeff Bezos reaches space in first crewed flight of rocket New Shepard.* ITV Online. https://www.itv.com/news/2021-07-20/amazon-billionaire-jeff-bezos-excited-ahead-of-blue-origin-flight-to-the-edge-of-space

Various (2021b). *UK police investigate racist abuse of England's football players after Euro 2020 loss.* Politico. https://www.politico.eu/article/fa-condemns-racist-abuse-of-englands-football-players-after-euro-2020-loss/

Young, N. J. (2018, August). Gay 'conversion therapy' in 'Cameron Post,' 'boy erased' is far from a thing of the past. *Huffington Post, 1.* https://www.huffingtonpost.com/ entry/opinion-conversion-therapy-movies_us_5b7f1e64e4b0348585fee692

Chapter 2

Imperium

For those who have recognised that this book has a #Imperium at the very beginning in the title, it is important for me to actually spend a couple of sentences exploring the meaning of this word and its importance to this topic area. Imperium is a Latin word; broadly it translates to 'the power to command, supreme power or absolute dominion' (Oxford Languages, 2012). For this particular text, *The Psychology of Supremacy*, this is the perfect word with which to underline the topic area that I am exploring in this volume.

To go into a little bit more detail, in Ancient Rome different types of power and authority were given different terms. Imperium though refers to the role of the state over the individual. This term therefore separates it out from say more mundane sorts of structures of family, of culture and so on, and actually talks very much to the dictator, the leader, the magistrate of local communities. For example, Richardson (1991) looked at how in the last century BC and the first century AD, the word imperium signified the power that magistrates, and others who were elected by the people to serve, held over their populations, with this power often ascending upwards to the Senate itself. As Richardson states, it was through the imperium and through the actions of the Senate and people designated to control them, that the imperial structures were established. These powers then filtered down to the inhabitants of the provinces and were then used as a form of control and to mitigate the drawbacks of being sub-imperial. Already in this exploration of the term, we see the hierarchical nature of a state as defined by the term imperium. Supremacy therefore suggests at its very basic level a hierarchy where power rotates upwards and is filtered downwards upon the other.

Pillars of Supremacy

Client Example

Liz was a 45-year-old woman of Afro-Caribbean descent who lived on a poor estate in Southeast London. She came into counselling whilst I was working for a service in the area, some 15 years ago. Her presenting issue was around the anxiety and the fear that she walked within her day-to-day

DOI: 10.4324/9781003313229-2

life. A single mother, she had three children, two boys and a girl of varying ages and she worked part-time for a charity in the local community, supplementing the rest of her income with Tax Credits.

Although our work was short-term, given that we had originally started with six sessions and I extended her work to 12, there was a lot to consider in the time that we worked together. Whilst I found working with Liz to be illuminating and exciting, it was also at times quite challenging, given some of the cultural experiences of supremacy which permeated our work.

It was Patricia Hills-Collins (2019) who posited the idea of a white supremacist, capitalist patriarchy. This powerful statement for her recognised that these three systems: racial, gendered, and cultural sat at the centre of an intersectional approach to the oppressions endured by the other. In conjunction with this, for Lorde (1984) the idea that identity is not one fixed point and is a number of different points all made up to create a composite hole, recognises that we are all far more complex beings than we often see in physical narratives around equality and diversity. What these two theorists, when placed alongside each other, recognised was that for any one identity I may hold, that I may also experience varying aspects of oppression based upon said identity.

For Liz, in my client example, the fact that she is both of colour and a woman suggests that she might also endure experiences of oppression based upon not just her gender but her race. Coupled with the fact that she lived in a deprived area of London, the class aspect of this should not be disentangled from the rest of the narrative around Liz's identity. This chapter, therefore, looks to consider this triumvirate of white supremacy, patriarchy, and capitalism, and how these systems which are created by man have worked hand in hand to oppress the many others under their auspices. The importance of understanding and exploring the historical context of these is not just to present a lesson in the history of our culture, but to lay down a platform upon which a better understanding of how entrenched these systems are for ourselves and for our clients may present itself. Only by then understanding those, and by walking on that broad base of knowing, can theorists then start to look at and explore the more psychological impact of these systems in our counselling and psychotherapy trainings and with our clients. The first of these will be a consideration of perhaps the oldest system of them all, patriarchy. This will be followed by a consideration of capitalism before we end this section with an exploration of issues around race and the construct of race.

To begin with, it should be clearly stated that these are socially constructed systems that have often tried to find meaning and relevance through the scientific but are more often than not routed a lot more in the philosophical (Harris, 2006; Neimeyer, 1998). The attempts, therefore, to root these in the scientific world have, at times, resulted in the greater oppression of those set outside these wheelhouses. So much so that our profession as counsellors and psychotherapists, and the healthcare services, have been complicit in the vilification, marginalisation, the over-medication or the misdiagnosis of individuals and whole groups.

A perfect example of this comes with the use of hysteria against women nearly 100 years ago in this country, whereby for a woman to express herself in an appropriate fashion a lot of the time, within a patriarchal environment (Lev Kenaan, 2021). This mere action, this attempt to speak up and speak out often against systems of the time was met with marginalisation, medication, and the diagnosing of women into isolation and shame.

It should also be noted that these systems have not only had a major impact upon the immediate categories that they are in connection with and this chapter, but upon many others. This chapter will therefore also explore the impact on the LGBTQ community of systems of oppression like patriarchy and white supremacy; upon the disabled of systems like capitalism and the patriarchy; and even explore the impact on the environment of not only capitalism but also patriarchy and white supremacy (Jacobs, 2003).

The other in these chapters is therefore not animate, it is not just human, it is animal, it is plant based, it is what one might term as inanimate. It is based upon systems that impact upon the world we live within, the wider reaches of which have psychological challenges for all of us. Supremacy is therefore far more widespread, far more nuanced and far more subtle than previously considered in governmental narratives. This does not mean it is not possible to challenge its position of priority because it is by the very fact of this book being written and published. Yet, what it does mean is that whilst living within said systems we are often not aware of the woods of oppression within which the systemic trees before us stand.

Patriarchy

On the evening of 3 March 2021, Sarah Everard, a 33-year-old marketing executive was kidnapped and murdered in South London while she was on her way home from visiting a friend's house in the area. Her murderer, Wayne Cousins, a police officer with the Metropolitan Police, was found guilty in October 2021 of her rape, strangulation, and murder. This incident raised the spectre of patriarchal violence against women in the United Kingdom, holding distinct echoes of the #MeToo movement in the United States and across the world. The murder of Sarah Everard led to vigils in and around towns and cities across the United Kingdom. The saddest part of some of these protests was the role take up by the police in certain areas, with often violent attempts being made to disperse what were peaceful, candlelit vigils to commemorate the murder of one woman, and to bring attention to the continued oppression of women across the country (Morton, 2021).

In their wonderful series of podcasts, Biewen (2018) from Scene on Radio explored the idea that patriarchy as a system is perhaps around 10,000 years old.

This is important, as it recognises that when we talk about something which people say does not exist, part of the reason why they believe it does not exist is because it is so old and so normalised that to question its existence is to literally questions the very experience of humanity.

Numerous theorists have considered how and why the patriarchy has taken such a hold. There have been ideas posited that as humanity moved from a more hunter gatherer means of sustaining itself to a more farming based way, that the idea of power and strength then became more prevalent and more necessary so that those who were physically stronger, such as men in these narratives, were then seen to hold higher value in said societies (Hawkes, 2020; Potts & Campbell, 2008). This movement to a more patriarchal society in the Global North is not mirrored in some cultures across the globe. In some First Nation cultures in the Americas where the system is set up on a more collective basis, whilst some men may have prominence, the role of the collective and in particular the role of women in making decisions for the collective good, has never been denied.

In the Global North, patriarchal narratives and experiences have governed the experiences and the lives of women from the times of the Ancient Greeks through to the Romans to the Middle Ages and the burning of witches at crosses, to the more modern times of the industrialised age where women in this country were not allowed to own land (Beauvoir, 2010). Many of the advances in the feminist fight for equality have come up in the past 150 years. For example, Emily Pankhurst and her quest for women's voting rights over 100 years ago is a very recent stage in the fight for women's rights in this country, a fight that actually at that stage was more about the rights of middle-class women than it was about those from the working class beneath them (Pugh, 2008). It was only when this fight was then continued by the likes of her daughter, Sylvia Pankhurst, that a more intersectional approach to women's rights was first attempted in this country.

Works such as *The Second Sex* by De Beauvoir (2010) and the work of Butler (1990) have added a more contemporary nuanced and broader vision of just what the oppression of women looks like in the modern era. These examples, though, speak very much from a westernised perspective on difference and otherness, and yet there are numerous other writers who have written extensively about feminism and the experience of living within a patriarchal environment. For example, Spivak (1988) writes about a very different cultural experience of feminism, and there have been numerous other papers from authors as far reaching places as Africa, the Far East, the Middle East and so on, in their explorations of cultural difference and the broader cultural context of feminism (Bannerji, 2000; Hancock, 2013; Ohito, 2019).

That women have had to endure being seen as second-class citizens to men is without question. Even within the American Constitution women were not included as part of that narrative towards equality, it was all about white men and patriarchy. Patriarchy though has never been just about the oppression of women. It also involves the oppression or the rejection of certain types of masculinity. The gay male experience, for example, has often been marginalised and in many cases illegalised in favour of a form of masculinity which is seen as 'normal' (Andersen, 2014; Sánchez & Vilain, 2012). This has gone so far that it was only in the mid-1960s that homosexuality in this country, the United Kingdom, was made legal, whilst the internalised attitudes towards homosexuality have remained within the culture.

Toxic masculinity (Haider, 2016) is also another factor or another player in the oppression experienced through the patriarchy. The ideas that men need to be a certain way, that they cannot express their feelings, but how they are seen has to fit in with some sort of pre-determined stereotypical vision of masculinity. This is a major factor in why so many men feel suicidal before the age of 25, and why the highest rates for suicide in men is between the ages of 45–49 (Office for National Statistics, 2014). A direct correlation to this is the increasing numbers of books in the modern era which detail what it is to be a man when one steps outside of this pre-determined macho attitude.

For example, the idea that there should be a female Doctor Who, a character, an alien, and therefore without gender, in a long running British television science fiction show, and that such a female character should be directly linked to the cause for male violence, shows the backlash when the gendered other steps out of the role designated for it by the patriarchy (Various, 2021c). That the patriarchy has had a huge hand in defining just what it is to be a man, as well as a woman, should therefore not be underestimated. That its ideas and systems are stretched out towards becoming political laws and norms, should also be part of this exploration. In my private practice, I have had numerous male clients who struggle with understanding what it is for them to be seen as masculine, given that how they want to be seen is often vilified and denigrated by their peers or their friends or others.

In my own experience, I remember when I joined the Royal Air Force in 1989 at the age of 19. My friends, other black men of the same age as myself, and some white, thought that I was flawed in some way, that maybe I was gay or that I did not understand what it was to be a black man because black men do not join the military. One friend of mine, years later though, who by then was working in the mental health services, subsequently said to me that he then understood why I had gone away and joined the military. He saw that many of the men that he worked with have for varying reasons collapsed under the weight of the psychological pressures to fit in with an idea of what black masculinity looked like. Their subsequent breakdowns having left them in some cases with a life of psychosis and psychological distress.

This is not to say that the inability to acknowledge the fullness of masculinity can lead one towards a breakdown. What it does start to point at is that with the externalised narratives of patriarchal supremacy, the idea that there is not only one way to be as man but there is a patriarchal power narrative which defines us all, can then become internalised for both men and for women to such an extent that we then subsequently cause ourselves psychological damage.

What I mean by this is that the internalisation of such a long-running and long-standing form of oppression is not just limited to men. The sheer number of women, who would have voted for someone as potentially misogynistic as Donald Trump, shows that no matter the reality that a good number of women will forgive the affairs, the numerous children, the disrespect towards women. Supremacy in these instances is not held up from within the circle, it is actually held up from those at its edges, no matter the failures and flaws of the figurehead. It is those acolytes around the fringes that will support said structure.

Patriarchal narratives have also influenced the disabled community. Ideas about what it is to be a man have had a detrimental impact upon those who are seen as other abled. From areas of understanding about neurodiversity to the projected ideals around children pre-birth, where there is a concern that a child may be born with an other ability. Patriarchal narratives have very much influenced the ideals that we project into the world about how we should be seen as human beings (Alim, 2010; Barnes, 2016; Mintz, 2017).

Another example is the impact that this had had upon the construction of the worlds around us, for example simple things like the ability to get from A to B, things which are very much denied to those who are other able bodied, has emerged out of a world which is not only ableist but is also quite patriarchal in its design. Patriarchy has placed itself, and in particular the men within it, at the forefront of any construction of the world and it is only within the last generation that there has been a greater effort to deconstruct the ableist patriarchal ideology which dominates the design and manufacture of our environment. From buses with ramps and drop ledges to pavements which allow the movement of wheelchairs from the raised position down on to the street below, to how we view the schooling of those who are labelled autistic or neurodiverse, given the positioning of those men in power to decide upon the worth of the disabled via their level of interaction with the rest of us, it has often been felt that those who are seen as other abled were not only marginalised but were often forgotten about (Kapp et al., n.d.; L. Richardson et al., 2016).

When we consider issues around ageism, patriarchal narratives and stereotypes have also played a huge role. The fact that, for example in the media, the cultural imaging of a strong man as being white, male, often blonde haired, or maybe dark haired as well, and of, say of middle age, has meant that those who are deemed to be older often find themselves marginalised and also in a similar vein to those from a more ableist perspective them find themselves forgotten about (Blytheway, 1995). The isms: ageism, ableism, racism, sexism and we can add in here homophobia, all have strands that tie themselves to the patriarchy. They are not solely constructed by such, as I will explore further on in this chapter, but they are all in some ways manipulated and often dominated by the patriarchy itself.

Client Example

Liz's relationships with men had problematic to say the least. Although all the three children were all from the same father, it appeared that he had never really committed to her, and the children and they had never really built a life together. This left Liz feeling quite resentful towards her ex-partner, aresentment that occasionally came into the space with myself as a man and as a black man. She had often heard from her own mother that black men were useless, that she should not rely on a black man at all; the narrative being that to look to one to support you was to be weak as they never stayed and they would never be there to support and care for their own children.

Whilst she was smart enough to recognise the historical cultural wounds that sit within the race, what she was also very wary of was of feeling anything less than superior or important to a black man. She had, though, recently started online dating, and had found herself very much drawn to a number of white men of better means. This she found intriguing, recognising that her own behaviour would change when with these men. Often she found herself feeling more secure, safer, happier even. Whilst some of these relationships had not lasted for very long, the gentleman she was with currently she had been dating for about six months.

In our relationship, Liz's fear that I knew more about her own process than she did was a common factor in our discussions. She found it sometimes difficult to find a voice in a room, as she stated herself, where she was sat with a man. This left her experiencing the internalised impact of patriarchal oppression.

As Carl Jung (1963) would state in his work on dreams, one of the main reasons for us to dream is that the dream acts in a fashion whereby it shows us how our unconscious self has become split off from its own reality. Liz's dreams would often involve her feeling quite angry or aggressive towards myself, or more often finding herself wanting to say things that she felt unable to say in the room. The projected imagery that I represented involved an idea that I was her internalised patriarch. Doing some Chair Work, from the Gestalt Therapy means of working meant the client had the chance to get in touch with both the patriarch and herself as the other (Maurer, 2012). This proved to be incredibly powerful in helping her to reconnect with the power that systemic oppression had robbed her of consciously. This process though was not one that was undertaken once and resolved instantly. As previously stated, given patriarchy thousand's years of existence, to try and even explore material like this where it creates change for a client, takes time and a willingness to not only observe the internalised impact of said oppression, but also to work with and discover a previously unrecognised and in some ways new, way of being.

To explain further, created by Perlz, Chair Work is a technique created from the Gestalt means of working (Cheung & Nguyen, 2012). The general idea is that clients would project aspects of their collective intersectional identity onto a chair opposite them, or onto more than one if need be. The client would then have the opportunity to then either embody each of these split-off aspects, or to relate to them, telling each of them maybe what they have always wanted to say or express. This creative (re)creation of a relationship with the internalised other then becomes a means of working with the unconscious other within us all.

So, for Liz, although this took time and continued practice, and although at times she would come back to re-silencing herself, she did so recognising that this repeated pattern involved her growing an awareness of what she had internalised and what in turn she was restarting to do to herself. This therefore shows how an ignorance of an understanding of the patriarchy and its cultural, political, and social influence on all our lives, then leaves us bereft of certain information when it comes to understanding our client's material.

White Supremacy

It should be stated from the beginning that my view of race and racism is that these are social and cultural constructs (T. Andrews, 2012; Schubert, n.d.). Whilst there have been numerous attempts to tie them to some sort of scientific basis, many of these have since been rightly debunked for the pseudo-scientific nonsense of the time they were embedded. A perfect example was the measuring of heads of those from African continents versus those from Europe and the idea that the larger the head the more intelligent one was (Biewen, 2017).

Pseudo-scientific ideas that there is a human basis for the construct of race have now only recently started to be deconstructed. The damage though has already been done. So, whilst when Bill Clinton (Various, 2000) clearly stated that the human genome for all of us on the plant is 99.9 per cent the same, ideas of race and racial difference go all the way back one might say to the sixteenth century when Infante D. Henrique when in 1455 Pope Nicholas V gave him advocacy and the rights to transport and enslave the lesser races of black people from Africa so they could be moved to the New World (Pereira, 2016).

White supremacy though is a tricky subject. It is often projected as if it is just about a colour. It is not. It is a system. A system of ideals for what it is to be a person who is white, a system outside of which many white groups have over times either been marginalised or continue to do so. For example, during the early days of slavery, there were slaves from the Celtic nations who were transported out to the New World and used in a similar vein to those from Africa. This, though changed subtly around the time of when slaves started to rebel and run away from harm, their whiteness thereby altering the legislation put in place with regard to how to punish the different races. What this soon came to mean was that those who were from the Celtic nations, because they were seen as close enough to white, were given lighter sentences to those who were seen as non-white. So much so, that the idea of whiteness involved the subsuming of those who were deemed to be closer to colour and nature and class and culture.

Racial constructions and white supremacy in the modern era still continue to marginalise certain groups. The traveller communities (Ahmed, 2007) for example are one group that are positioned outside of traditional aspects of whiteness. Eastern Europeans who are not considered to be black are actually considered to be not white enough in some ways, their marginalisation including restricting their ability to come to the United Kingdom and work. These and other 'white communities' have often experienced marginalisation when European countries enter into their isolationist and populist phases, and was particularly apparent when the United Kingdom removed itself from the European Union with Brexit (Boffey, 2018; Khomami, 2016).

The most infamous example of the structures of whiteness taking a firm hold is probably with the rise of Nazism in Germany, whereby this ideal of whiteness was taken to its most logical/illogical conclusion in the creation and an idealisation of an Aryan race (Stanley, 2018). The white skinned, blonde haired, blue eyed masculine man also held within itself ideals of the patriarchy. Men were very much still gifted positions of power, but only certain men were allowed to ascend to the very highest echelons, whereas women were often relegated to secondary roles. So, what we start to see in these discussions is the crossover, the intersections of both patriarchy and white supremacy. This is why as Hill Collins (Collins, 2019) has previously stated, an intersectional approach not only broadens the discussions around explorations of difference and otherness and supremacy but recognises the complex interwoven web of oppressions that we live with both culturally outside of ourselves and that we also inevitably internalise as we survive this plain of existence.

The link between white supremacy and capitalism will be explored further on, but it is already worth noting, for example that within the colonial projects that existed around the world, the ideas of supremacy are what has led to the annihilation of indigenous Americans during the invasion of the Americas after the arrival of Christopher Columbus. In the more modern era, given the nature of white supremacy and given how it has existed for hundreds of years, this initial structure of supremacy has now evolved so that it influences many different systems, organisations, and institutions that we exist within, or that rotate around us every day.

When George Floyd was murdered in May 2020, his death sent reverberations around the varying non-white communities across the world (Various, 2020). Witnessing on social media and online a white policeman's knee on the neck of a black man, the voyeuristic annihilation of one man brought with it the re-traumatising of millions if not billions of persons of otherness across the planet, myself included. Protests were held, many of which were against the rise of white supremacy; many of which called out the systems of oppression that they had endured during colonial times and post then. Here in the United Kingdom, where the protests were different, as statues were toppled this government pushed back against the idea that there was any form of racism within their organisations and their culture as explored in the Channel Four Documentary, Has George Floyd Changed Britain (2021d).

When the British Government produced its Seely Report in spring of 2021, this report ran counter to numerous others in its statement that the United Kingdom was not institutionally racist and that class was a greater indicator of inequalities than race was (Commission on Race and Ethnic Disparities, 2021). That this report was then castigated by the United Nations who themselves said that a report such as this would lead to the promotion of white supremacy, shows just how far reaching and how deep the struggle is for power and control in this particular country (Merrick & White, 2021). Another example in the United States came with the loss of the election of Donald J. Trump at the end of 2020 and the subsequent riots on Capitol Hill in early January 2021, riots promoted by supremacist organisations across the Atlantic (Various, 2021f). Yet, for President Biden to call out white supremacy as a major problem in America, whilst admirable fails to recognise the systemic problem that we all have and how, like the ends of an enormous spider's web these little slithers infect and connect into every aspect of the world we live within (Singh, 2021).

Another example for how white supremacy maintains its prominent position came at the end of 2020 in a strange story which involved the BBC (2020) and their attempts to stop people from singing Rule Britannia during the British cultural event which is the Proms. From the very highest echelons of the BBC, apparently, a message came out saying in support of issues of racism within the culture they would find other ways to celebrate British culture without singing said song. Following this announcement, numerous far right narratives or diatribes came out calling this out as political correctness having gone too far. They rejected such a claim and demanded that this song be reinstituted as a symbol of the strength of the United Kingdom. On television shows though, persons of colour were invited in to talk about the problems in having a song like this played on national television. During lots of these discussions, these persons of colour were often castigated by their co-presenters or by other members of the panel. The interesting thing about this whole narrative, this whole story, is its systemic presentation of the power of whiteness. What I mean by this is that post the murder of George Floyd persons of colour were not walking the streets collectively asking for the BBC to stop singing Rule Britannia. What they were actually asking for was an end to the systemic violence meted out against them. This tokenising of a response by a major corporation then became the baiting of a right-wing narrative which actually in the end re-enforced a position of white supremacy. So again we see that actually for persons of colour there is not the need to do very much because often times, as spotted by the likes of Stuart Hall, Martin Luther King and James Baldwin, it is the political left in their passive aggression around race and difference that will often act in an even more insidious fashion in the reinforcement of white supremacy (Baldwin, 2017; Durant, 1994; Proctor, 2004).

Client Example

Issues of race though were where Liz felt most comfortable in talking to myself. Liz saw the issues of race that would come up in her previous relationships with white man, as often they would objectify or exotify her, something that she hated and yet occasionally also found comfort within. Whilst at work, the micro aggressions of one colleague meant that she often felt less than said colleague and some of her other peers in the workplace. These were things she felt most comfortable talking to myself about, assuming that we had the same cultural and racial background, that we ate the same food, spoke with the same patois and made the same jokes. She would often find comfort in knowing that, although I was a counsellor and although I was seen by her to be somebody who was in a different class because of my profession, racially she also felt able to relate to me and a modicum of safety in said relationship.

For Liz, when it came to supremacy, a lot of our work involved exploring how living as a woman of colour in white environments meant that she often felt unseen or stereotyped, sometimes at exactly the same time. Liz told me a story whereby she was at work, and she had tried to stand up for herself with her colleagues, one of whom had burst into tears and said that she was being overly aggressive, and she needed to watch her tone when relating to her. The reason for Liz to express herself had actually been quite a reasonable one, involving a request to be able to leave a little bit early for a doctor's appointment, something that she had witnessed other colleagues doing on numerous occasions. The level of tone policing though, and the passive aggression of her peers in the workplace, aspects that she knew were already there, meant that she already found it very difficult to say what she needed to say. It was our work together that helped her to recognise that this internalisation and a reality in that she was working in an environment where she would be seen as something to be feared, meant that it was very hard for her to find a voice in such a challenging space.

That she was then doubly impacted by having spoken up and been told that she was said stereotype, meant that she felt ashamed and angry, not just of having had such an impact but of feeling that it was not OK for her to ask for her need to be met in the work environment. In some ways, what had happened for this client echoes Diangelo's (2018) work around the white fragility of her colleagues. To broaden out such a topic even further or to deepen it perhaps, ideas of fragility involved the anonymity and the silencing and the invisibility of blackness in relation to its co-created companion which is whiteness. The shadow, in this case blackness, has to remain invisible, whilst the ego, that which is of whiteness in this instance, must remain prominent, dominant, and supreme.

The most important part of this exploration though in my work with Liz was in helping her to understand that the shame that she felt at being pushed back into the shadows was not actually her own (Wigger, 2010). Supremacy works on the premise that the other is less human, has fewer needs and thereby should not receive the same level of care as that which is deemed at the centre, in this case whiteness. Supremacy also works by injecting any sense of shame into the now invisible other so that it its egoic state can remain cocooned in its own system of specialness unimpacted by anything negative it might have done to said other.

As we unpacked the shame that Liz was left with, and as I helped her to understand that this was not her own, she then started to feel better able to request again that which she would like from her colleagues. This time, though it was less about actually achieving said goal but more about saying what she needed to say, being heard and then letting the chips lie whichever way they fell. The difficulty for those of otherness when faced with the unconscious supremacy of whiteness in this instance is that there is an expectation that the subject must meet said needs and that if they do not then there is no need to speak up, to say anything, to do anything at all. This is flawed, because what that suggests is that the two are inexorably tied together, that any responsibility that the slave might have to borrow Hagel's point, is deferred to said master as Fanon might echo (Fanon, 2005; Hegel, 1976). The other must feel re-energised in its right to express itself. The other must recognise its own power. Yet, the other must also recognise the limitations of said powerless it itself fall into the trap of internalising its needs to be supreme.

This last aspect is actually quite important and is something that I will explore further on in this book. Basically, it involves the idea that for a system of supremacy to reconstitute itself, what often happens through traumatic experiences is that any fear of going back to said space as an outsider or as a victim, then drives the projection of said victim outwards onto an alternative other.

Capitalism

This third aspect, capitalism, is perhaps not only one of the most modern forms of oppression, relatively speaking, but also one of the most insidious and destructive for us as a collective. Capitalism at its core is driven by a need for financial supremacy. Class systems, both here in the United Kingdom and in the United States and across Europe are riven with inequality as derived from capitalism. So much so, that governments have worked hard in my view, to deconstruct any sort of narrative which might protect those of the working classes so that profits can be maintained and increased accordingly by those who have worth (Procter, 2004).

One of the major contemporary experiences where capitalism has perhaps maintained itself and enhanced itself, has actually been during the pandemic called COVID-19. A virus which seems to have originated out of China around 2019, this incredibly destructive illness has, at the time of writing, led to the infection of 270,000,000 people worldwide, and the deaths of 5,500,000 (as per the 1st of December 2021). A considerable number of these deaths have been here in the United Kingdom, in the United States and across Europe, where for example 800,000 people have died in the United States, and 145,000 in the United Kingdom. Some of these incredibly high death tolls are in countries where capitalism is most prevalent and most embedded. At first glance it would seem strange to believe that these countries, these wealthy nations, will be the ones with the highest levels of deaths and infection rates for the whole world. But what this also shows is a few underlying factors which are important to recognise. Across the Global North, whilst this virus has attacked whole communities without compunction, what it has also shown up is how the levels of inequality have led to increased rates of infection amongst certain communities. In the early stages of the COVID-19 pandemic in the United Kingdom, the rate of infections and death amongst black communities and Asian communities was around twice the rate as compared to those of white communities (British Psychological Society, 2020).

Whilst stay at home policies, or lockdowns, were instituted whereby huge swathes of the population of the western world were encouraged to stay indoors, for those from those poorer backgrounds remaining indoors in often cramped high rise conditions, was an added form of oppression which actually did little more than to increase psychological distress at home (Heejung, 2020). This contrasted greatly to a slow but ongoing movement of those who had funding and had money and were able to move themselves from their primary workplaces and homes in major towns to live out in the countryside or make use of garden areas whereby they had the space to manage the psychological impact of lockdowns (Prados-Ojeda et al., 2021).

Another layer of this involved the interesting phenomena of hoarding of goods when the pandemic first occurred. In many places, and many nations, the shelves within major shops were cleaned out of most basic goods. Anything from toilet roll to pasta to tinned goods was bought up and taken away in a sort of binge shopping frenzy not seen for several generations. This hoarding mentality, this primal instinctual need for survival was also managed by the ability of those who had money to actually do exactly this. This contrasted though to efforts to support those people, often children from poorer backgrounds, whose parents were already relying on food banks (Sydney, 2020).

Here in the United Kingdom, when the footballer Marcus Rashford petitioned government to actually provide support for children during the pandemic, children who were off school and whose only meals of the day would often be those provided by said schooling system, the government of this country was reluctant to even implement a system whereby these children would be supported (Various, 2021a). Their critiques, nay attacks, on Mr Rashford ranging from a form of silencing, whereby he was told that as a footballer you should not have a voice on politics to a sort of racialised white supremacy, whereby the idea was that they knew better, and he should just stay in his lane. The fact that Mr Rashford's point is actually a moral one, seemed to be missed by many of those in power.

This is how capitalism in many ways, much like any other form of supremacy, works. It ignores the moral inner requirement to move towards equity and promotes an ideological positioning of one group of humans over another group of said humanity. Supremacy has also though in the modern era led to the destruction, the rape and pillaging of the planet that we live upon. During 2021 a report commissioned by the United Nations (IPCC, 2021) stated categorically that climate change was primarily driven by humanity's exploitation of the environment, a report that stated that this drive for wealth means the destruction of the planet has gone so far that in some areas, and in some ways, it is now irreversible. The use of fossil fuels, the manufacturing and discarding of plastics, the annihilation of whole species of animals, are just some of the ways in which our need and our greed have left our very environment in distress and our very existence as human beings at risk. That this harsh existential crisis is occurring at the same time as private companies and billionaires fly themselves into space, shows how capitalism has neglected in its moral obligation to look after the other, in this case the planet. To underline this Cianconi et al. (2020) provided an excellent paper whereby they measured the impact of climate change upon the mental health of the those in their 20s. What they found was an increase in what is termed, climate anxiety, whereby their participants expressed that their mental health was suffering because of what they witnessed as the destruction of the planet and increasing levels of climate change.

The exploitation of an other for gain, is of course not just limited to the planet. That huge swathes of the human population have at times been utilised as part of this capitalist project, if in other guises, is another symptom of the supremacy of capitalism. For example, Queen Victoria led the colonial project through the United Kingdom signing off on its own part of what was to become the Transatlantic Slave Trade (Moore, 2010). The movement was initially propagated by the Spanish and the Portuguese who saw profit in taking cheap labour from the African subcontinent and transporting it across to the New World whereby slaves would be used to colonise and mine the New World for its resources. Queen Victoria and the British in many ways took this drive a stage further and the European slave trade led to the movement of between 10 and 12 million slaves to the New World (Akbar, 1984). This exploitation, the renaming and the abuses all in the name of profit, sat central within a trade that moved as far north as North America and into Canada and as far south as down into Brazil and Argentina. The sheer scale of the project to colonise the Americas for profit is something that earned the Western powers an indescribable amount of income; income derived from the kidnapping of slaves and the collective genocide of many indigenous cultures already resident on said continents. These included and were not limited to the indigenous Americans in the north of America whose losses are often quoted to be between 50 and 60 million people, where small numbers still now fight for survival (Dudley, 2017). This contrast to South America, where many of the cultures that had existed for thousands of years found themselves utterly wiped out by the superior forces of the colonisers (Cesarino, 2012; Kingsford-Smith, 2014).

The colonial project is something that, as I am sure we all understand by this stage, existed across the world from India to Australia and New Zealand, with the European powers establishing themselves with varying footholds for the goods and services thereby on offer. As we are beginning to see, one key facet of colonialism was the destruction of many groups of people resident in said nations. For example, King Leopold II of Belgium was the mastermind behind the genocide in the Congo that cost the lives of around 10 million slaves who were used to mine the said the country for its major products including rubber. Punishments meted out to those deemed to have transgressed or not met targets, included the loss of limbs, and other such atrocities including death (H. S. King & Ghost, 2011).

The colonial project has more recently seen the uncovering of unmarked graves in Canada attached to schools whereby the children of indigenous Canadians were sent in order to be rid of the primitive side of their nature as deemed by the colonisers (Unknown, 2021). The graves though marked out the atrocities that these children endured at the hands of those who were tasked with their care, the types of which we will sadly and perhaps thankfully, never know the reasons behind and the full extent of. All we can imagine is that these hundreds of children at varying sites across Canada endured horrific treatments at the hands of their colonisers and supposed carers.

In a similar vein, in Australia children were taken away from their Aboriginal homes and taken to schools to be educated to be English (Various, 2019b). The colonial project in its softer, but no less destructive form, has led the minds of many a Caribbean child being colonised pre the end of the Commonwealth, left behind in the Caribbean to live with grandparents and other relatives. This was all whilst their actual parents left to come and build a better life in the United Kingdom, often seduced by the belief that they would be regarded as truly English because they spoke the Queen's English taught in their schools, because they drank Earl Grey Tea, and because they watched cricket on a Saturday afternoon (Thomas, 2000).

The internalised and transgenerational cost of colonialism as a facet of capitalism for those who have been made slaves or been seen as less than is something which resonates through culture to today. For example, when considering DeGruy's (2005) work around post-traumatic slave syndrome, the internalised self-deprecation of blackness when faced with the power of the coloniser. It is enormous in that it is often, for example, safer to be seen as self-deprecating and therefore non-threatening, than it is to be seen as any sort of challenge for those of whiteness and of colonial power. This is often an aspect which is not considered when one tries to understand the unconscious impact of living under systemic supremacy; that individuals and groups will often struggle to extricate themselves from the impact of said system, its internalisations often acting out from the shadowy confines of the unconscious. Simultaneously, for those who hold supremacy, whilst they may be well meaning, their behaviours will often adhere and reinforce the edicts of the system they are embedded within.

This is something which is seen in the behaviour of organisations and institutions to this day, such as the police, the British National Health Service, and any institution designed to govern in that those who are deemed as other are often treated more harshly than those who are seen to be of the culture inherent. Obvious examples emerge from stop and search reports which state that the rate of stop and search of those persons of colour is around eight times greater than those identified as white, and three times more than those identified as Asian (Various, 2021b). Or, how the rate of institutionalisation for those of colour in mental health institutions is more than four times that for white patients (Independent Review of the Mental Health Act, 2018; Various, 2019a). Or even, the number of cases whereby women of colour die in childbirth in the United Kingdom is sometimes conservatively posted at four times greater than for those of white women (Summers, 2021).

These sorts of statistics are just some examples utilised to outline the deeper levels of supremacy central to the institutions that the other must engage within in order to feel safe and contained within said environments. Whereas I could have produced numerous other examples, what is important to recognise is that these are not isolated cases and that supremacy, whilst it is deemed to be not just of whiteness and of patriarchy, is also constructed around the capitalist narrative that runs back hundreds of years and has its ties to empire, colonialism, the Commonwealth. Supremacy also internationally is a face of the systemic structures that underpin some of the major worldwide superpowers such as the United States of America and the former Soviet Union who had in their own ways, both tried to establish their own colonial projects.

Other examples of colonial projects include Mussolini's invasion of Ethiopia in the 1930s which led to the exile of His Royal Highness Haile Selassie II here to the United Kingdom and the German attempts to establish their own sort of colonial project in East Africa; their invasion meaning they established settlements in places such as Tanzania. The now legendary

Partition of Africa which was held in Berlin in 1844 and involved the carving up by the western nations of Africa is in itself a form of supremacy in the belief that said countries had the right to own and possess the African other. These are not isolated incidents.

Client Example

Liz had come to a service which was free to access, and she felt a great deal of shame about this, feeling that she should be able to afford to attend a better service with trained fully qualified counsellors and psychotherapists. She had gone to university, had got herself a BA in business, but had always struggled to find herself a position whereby she could move up the ladder, giving up working when she had the first of her children.

We talked about the impact of coming from a working-class background and living on one of the poorest estates in London, and Liz broke down and cried when she talked about the shame of this and how she would not only struggle to provide for herself, but she had often sacrificed her own needs for those of her children. For example, giving up on meals just so that her three children were fed and looked after. This was something she found difficult to discuss with myself, perceiving me as being better off, given that I was working as her counsellor.

We also considered the envy that she had towards some of her peers where she worked, being the only woman of colour in the charity where she was employed amongst several other women, a couple of whom were obviously from middle class backgrounds. This envy often turned to resentment for Liz, something that she also felt quite ashamed of because she knew this was not down to them or her, it was just a matter of circumstance and coincidence that they had all found themselves working in the same space together.

Liz recognised that many of the ideas she held were passed down to her by her parents who, although from the Caribbean, had come to this country at around the time of the end of the empire. This meant that she had imbibed many of the teaching passed to said parents and grandparents as a means not just of education, but more so of control. Liz found it very difficult to express herself, not just out of racialised means, not just because her colleagues were white and middle class, but because she had been taught by her parents about the power dynamics inherent in any interaction with those middle class while women. This was particularly painful for her because she had done a good amount of reading over the years in exploring what a colonised mind might look like, but it was only with our work that we were able to see just how far and how deep the intersecting layers of white supremacy and in this case capitalism cloaked in colonialism, had gone in silencing such a powerful woman (as I saw her). Helping her to find her voice, therefore, was not just about ridding herself of the internalised supremacist, it was also about returning to her the power and the authority to be more in relationship with said women.

Another facet of this, was the fact that in her financial struggles through life, it was apparent that she had always under-achieved. She earned enough money to support herself to a certain level, but often found that she needed the additional funds given to her by the government to top up her monthly budget. When we looked at what it might be like for her to not just be more but to earn more, the level of shame, the level of internalised embarrassment that came up for her was quite palpable in the room. The struggle for this client to recognise that as powerful black women, that it was OK to even attempt to earn the amount of money that her peers in her workplace were earning became so alive for Liz that in one session she talked about the following dream that she had had a couple of nights previously.

The dream involved Liz living in Leeds. While she was there, she found herself walking up the road to go to one of the local market stalls to buy some vegetables and a bit of meat in order to make her Saturday Caribbean stew. When she got to the top of the road, she turned left and as she walked to one of the stores, she saw that the road was full of numerous cars and buses all busily making their way down the road itself. All of a sudden, these cars pulled to the side of the road. Liz then stepped out to the edge of the road to try and understand why. She realised that somebody was coming down the road in a car. As the car approached, she saw that it was a large, black Jaguar car and as it drove slowly down the road, she saw that within the car was a famous white woman that she had admired from afar (and had also admired in real life as she often appeared on television). Liz found herself comparing herself to this woman as she drove past and being amazed by the quiet that existed as the car progressed down the road. This then transformed back so the road became bustling again once the car had passed.

In working with the dream, there are many key facets that were quite important, but one of the most important was helping the client to recognise that in Jungian terms she was not only the woman in the car, but that she was also the car itself (R. A. Johnson, 1986; D. Turner, 2016b). There was power; there was grace; there was a slight colonised feel as it was a Jaguar car, but then there was also a woman who earned her way and had her own level of power and authority and presence.

Working creatively with Liz and with her internalised perception as the other, helped her to recognise that she had also internalised a sense that she was less than in the comparison with this famous woman in the car. It was only when she could step into said car, drive said car, and be said woman would she start to embody and be the powerful woman that she could be. So, what happened over time in our relationship is that using active imagination techniques designed by Jung we worked with this dream, with these images, time and again (Jung, 1997). As we worked with these images and she became the famous woman in the car, Liz took on the qualities of this woman in the car, transforming these into something which was more culturally appropriate for her. So, as we looked at the qualities the woman in the car held, and Liz found herself able to step out from under the safe, capitalist awning of working in a charity shop and fully embody the psychology degree that she had held for five years and not really felt she could do anything with. The power of capitalism and of an internalised sense of less than, and therefore of lack, was being challenged through our work together. Although Liz was never destined to be as rich as the famous woman driving the Jaguar, it was within her reach to be and own more.

Intersections of Supremacy

The importance of now understanding how the varying strands of supremacy have come into being then leads us to be able to start to explore where they intersect and where, when we follow one route, we ignore varying others, and therefore we reconstitute layers of oppression for different groups, both willingly but more often than not unwillingly.

It is important, therefore, to give you a particular example. Sylvia Pankhurst was born in 1882 in Manchester, to her mother Emmeline Pankhurst, the famous feminist and activist who led the Suffragettes in their fight for the rights of women here in the United Kingdom (Pugh, 2008). Sylvia Pankhurst's story though, although told as one of the core pillars of the feminist movement, struggles to recognise that certain groups of women were left out from the victories that she gained, especially in those early stages. For example, the fight for women's rights back between 1890 and 1919 actually became the fight for the rights of what would be termed middle class women to have the same rights as their husbands within a capitalist and patriarchal environment.

Sylvia Pankhurst though recognised that taking her own privilege, and using it to the best of her ability, would involve fighting not just for the rights of women, but also the rights of other disadvantages groups. Sylvia Pankhurst took up the fight for workers' rights in this country so much so that she was often arrested under the Cat and Mouse laws of the day, laws which involved a constant fight with the authorities as to whether or not she was fit to be incarcerated along with her peers (Pankhurst, 1979; Pugh, 2008). During these moments in prison, often times the unions, those of the working classes, would endeavour to band together and provide the funding and resources to either have her removed from prison or to support her fight in the courts (Pankhurst, 1979).

Sylvia Pankhurst also used her privilege to travel to the former Soviet bloc where she worked with and talked with a number of activists, politicians and artists, many of whom subsequently lost their lives in Stalin's purges. Finally, just as the Second World War was beginning, Sylvia Pankhurst took it upon herself to petition the British Government to enable them to bring to this country His Royal Highness Haylie Selassie the former Emperor of Ethiopia, as Mussolini's fascists fought to invade Ethiopia in their attempt to set up their own colonial project.

The reason I tell a story of a white feminist like Sylvia Pankhurst is not to suggest that she is an early forerunner of intersectional feminism. It is to point out that actually what this woman had done, this incredible, courageous, moral woman, had taken upon herself to do, was to use her skills, her abilities, and her privilege to fight not just against the patriarchy, but also against the capitalism of the time and also against the white supremacy that was embedded within the fascism that raged across Europe between the Second World War.

This is hugely important to recognise. When we look at intersectionality and when we tie it to the systems of oppression which are laid out there, what we also have to recognise is that it is very easy for any one of us to take up one singular fight and believe that that is the only form of oppression out there. It is not. It never has been, and it probably never will be. It is also important to recognise that our failure to recognise the intersectional nature of these systems of oppression could well mean that as well-meaning and feminist as one might be, that one may also be either consciously or unconsciously a white supremacist or a capitalist and be offending and oppressing a huge swathe of the population. It is not unheard of for feminists to be accused of homophobia or transphobia for example. There are numerous stories in the world today that highlight this (Bachmann & Gooch, 2017; Bettcher, 2014).

Another angle is that it is not unusual for a Person of Colour to fight for the rights of other POCs, and yet still create environments in their own communities whereby sexism and homophobia is rife and in some ways is even more insidious than out within the majority culture. It is also not uncommon to witness those are the forefront of the fight for LGBTQ+ rights, to be an activist stood on the front lines of Pride, and yet still watch many of those same persons marginalise others based upon race or class and such. Yet another perfect example of this whole system of oppressor versus oppressed was emergent out of the Brexit debate, whereby those of the working classes who understandably and obviously felt marginalised within their own countries, still had their own racism politically activated and used against them to such a degree that this country, the United Kingdom subsequently voted to leave the Economic Union.

An intersectional approach to supremacy, therefore, does not just broaden the ideas and narratives around systems of oppression that we all inhabit, but it also helps to broaden the systems that our clients walk within on a regular basis. Returning to my client example of Liz, the reason why I split it into three different sections within this book was just to highlight the differing angles that the work needed to approach. When we overlayer this, we start to see that these systems, these interlocking interplays of systems, are really quite difficult and insidious to unpick and unravel for any of us, and yet they are not impossible.

It is important, therefore, to recognise that for our clients and also for ourselves, any movement to resist the oppressive nature of one system may also lead to a reactivity whereby the other systems fill in the gaps subsequently left behind them. It is a bit like when you drop a pebble into a puddle, the hole the pebble creates as it descends and hits the base of the pond does not stay there; it is closed over, even if the water rises. We are therefore constantly in a conscious and unconscious battle with ourselves, much like our clients are, as we strive to understand these internalised aspects of oppression which need to be worked through and not projected outwards onto the other.

In the previous book in this series, the idea of projection played a massive role in understanding systems of oppression and how the other is created (von Franz, 1980). This is taken a stage further as we start to understand that these interlocking intersectional systems form a massive part of a superionic hierarchy which therefore worked well together to keep the ego in check. I am very aware at this point, in this second chapter, that I am offering a dialogue which enters into the world of psychotherapy but before gathering more pace around this in the third chapter, there is a great deal more ground to explore around just what supremacy is.

Supremacy, therefore, is not just whiteness. Supremacy is a system of oppression which overrides all others. It is a system of valuing oneself and devaluing the other, that has existed for thousands of years and, whilst it is difficult to see, it is not so difficult to understand and recognise its impact upon each and every one of us. As well as this, supremacy is a system which we are all infected by. From the day we are born, be us women born into wealthy families with a patriarchal structure or gay men and lesbian women born into families which are quite religious, these systems shape who we are and how much we can be of ourselves. Supremacy is universal, it is archetypal, and it needs to be understood more fully before we can get anywhere near starting to explore just how this archetype can be recognised, harnessed, and owned.

Exploring Conscious and Unconscious Supremacy

Conscious Supremacy

One of the major factors that I note now when considering supremacy, is that it sits in the space of social constructions of identity. Whilst there are, for example, biological constructions say of gender, those biological constructions do not state that one gender is superior to another, they just state they are different. That there are different cultural groups around the planet does not state that one group is better than another, they just state that those groups are different and, whilst there may be different sexualities of peoples around the planet, and whilst these might be genuine and true, there is no scientific reason as to why one sexuality is deemed better than another.

The social constructions which often infect and therefore impact upon these natural constructs of difference, change their perspectives totally. So a patriarchal influence on the construct of gender therefore manipulates that to a position whereby one gender is better and one gender is worse. To where a social influence on the construct of culture therefore becomes one of race and within that a building up of a social construct of race where one is positioned as better, or closer to God, than the other. The ideas and ideologies of superiority and inferiority then start to infect and impact upon both parties in said social construct; or where the social constructions which influences and impacts sexuality therefore changes how we view sexuality to one whereby one is seen as superior to another, to such an extent that certain forms of sexual identity need to be repressed and hidden away, with others designated as the more dominant, so they are positioned as superior and therefore desirable. The *Psychology of Supremacy* therefore recognises that it is the social construct of identity which therefore lead us to believe that one is better than another. Supremacy is therefore not a universal idea. It is a socially constructed one that influences all of our psychologies.

To say more about the social constructs of identity, I need to bring a couple of ideas to this book. The first is this, using race as an example, race is not a singular construct. As I have previously stated ideas of race have little to no basis within science (Jackson & Turner, 2021; D. Turner, 2021). At its essence, race is a binary social construct whereby whiteness identifies itself by blackness as a means of saying what it is and what it is not. This holds distinctive echoes of De Beauvoir's (2010) ideas around the social construct of gender, in that again ideas of what it is to be woman was decided and identified by what it was to be man, so whatever men believed themselves to be was cast out and projected onto woman accordingly.

Social constructs of identity are exactly that, they are social, they are relational, they are one plus another; they are not built-in isolation. This contrasts to the biological construct of say gender is not built man to woman, they just are: this is what a woman is, this is what a man is. The social constructs of man to woman are man first, this is what I am as a man, this is what I am not, therefore that is woman. They are built to mirror each other.

The second part of this discussion that needs to be recognised actually emerges from a book by Rousseau (1998) entitled *The Social Contract*. Jean-Jacques Rousseau's book, a classic of its time, recognised the philosophy behind social contracts and the idea that when we come into life we buy into, or we metaphorically sign, a social contract that therefore places us within a certain position within the world around us. So for example, if I am born into a working class family, I then will take on the social contract of what it means to be working class. It may well mean that I do not get to go to the best schools, but I accept that. It may well mean that I live with parents who are working al. he time and therefore I am a latch key kid, but in some ways, I accept that as well. It may well mean that I am not able or do not allow myself to have friends from a different social or class structure that might be higher than mine, but again I may well choose to accept that.

These parts of the unconscious social contract that Rousseau intimates dominate us. They actually involve the building up of a socially constructed armour of identity that we can sit within and be seen as. This therefore means that as a working-class boy from West London, when one says 'Oh, I'm working class', then those from a different class, or from a different area of town, or from a different city, or a different culture will automatically have their stereotypical ideas about that identity confirmed to them. In a way, I could suggest that Rousseau's ideas about the social contract, and how we adhere to those contractual ideas about identity, are actually a form of self-othering. My linking idea here is that in order to fulfil our part in this contract we give up our natural potential to be the fullest that we are in order to fit in and comply with a way of being that makes us non-threatening or that gives us comfort in some way (D. Turner, 2016a).

It is also worth noting though, that the social contract has a downside when it comes to the work that we do as counsellors and psychotherapists. Often in our trainings I will encounter students who struggle with the cultural identity they have been given within environments which are either predominantly male or predominantly middle class. Students often find themselves split between wanting to speak up and have a voice like their peers versus the contract which states that they must be quiet and know their place in order to not impact or infect the group dynamic. I often have to say that our courses are really just a microcosm of the culture that they live within, so the ability to adapt and to self-other for certain groups at certain times on said courses, is going to be as massive a factor within the courses as it would be for them in their outside environments where they walk on a day to day, week to week, month to month, year to year basis.

So, whilst we have considered the systemic nature of supremacy in the three main forms, it is also important to actually start to explore just how these forms then filter into other ways that supremacy can present itself. Figure 2.1 outlines a good, and yet not inexhaustible, number of ways that supremacy might present, both in society and therefore on our trainings and in our counselling and psychotherapy rooms.

To start to explore this diagram, it is wise to consider not just the triangular nature, but the first thing is that above the central line where conscious and unconscious meet at the very top, there are the three forms of supremacy that we have looked at thus far in this book, *Capitalism, White Supremacy,* and *Patriarchy.* There is though a fourth and that is *Religious Supremacism,* a topic which, within itself, is truly enormous and therefore beyond the remit of

PATRIARCHY

CONSCIOUS
SUPREMACY

WHITE
SUPREMACY

CAPITALISM

RELIGIOUS SUPREMACISM

FACISM

SOCIALISM

THINGIFICATION

HETERONORMATIVITY

MALE
ENTITLEMENT

CLASS
ENTITLEMENT

RACISM

SEXISM

CLASSISM

HOMOPHOBIA

ABLEISM

AGEISM

GREENWASHING

GAY/TRANS FEAR

WHITE
SYMPATHY

HIMPATHY

CLASS
SYMPATHY

POLITICS OF
INTEGRATION

DENIAL OF
DIFFERENCE

POLITICS OF
ASSIMILATION

UNCONSCIOUS
SUPREMACY

WHITE-
SPLAINING

MANSPLAINING

THE MYTHICAL
PAST/TRADITIONALISM

HISTORICAL
ERASURE

CULTURAL
APPROPRIATION

TOKENISM

TONE POLICING

IMPOSTER SYNDROME

MICROAGGRESSIONS

SILENCING

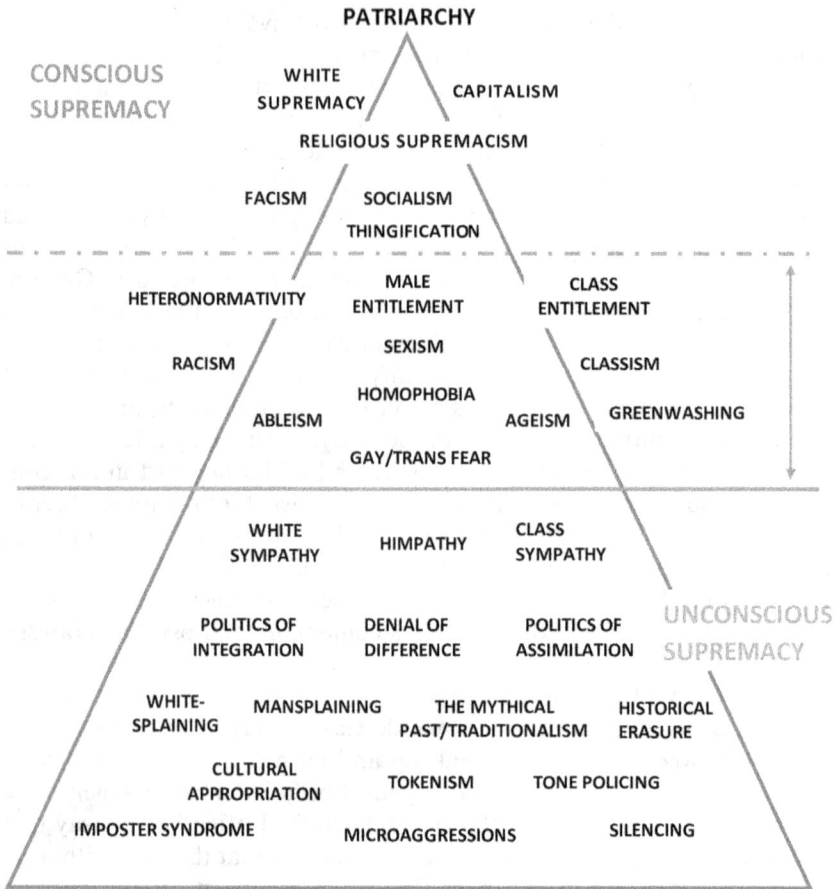

Figure 2.1 Conscious and Unconscious Supremacy.

this book at this stage. It is important though to recognise that it plays a huge role in re-enforcing and underpinning the other three forms of supremacy themselves, hence its position at the base of that top triangle. Briefly, religious rules have been used to reinforce and restate the position of men in relation to women in varying communities across the planet. Religious rules have been used to oppress and minoritise those persons of colour and LGBTQ minorities through a patriarchal misreading of the bible and so on. Religious supremacism has also been used to reinforce the cultural demands of capitalism, for example and the positioning of one culture's needs as being God given over the rights often of those indigenous populations upon whose land the colonisers have invaded.

Religious Supremacism is a massively powerful force in the oppression of other groups. It should also be clearly stated that we are not talking about religion, but what we are talking about is the interpretation of certain religious doctrines that have then been misused by the patriarchy. This means both those in charge of white supremacy, and by those who sit at the pinnacle of a capitalist system. So much so that these rules, when misused, have then had a direct impact upon numerous others beneath.

It should also be noted that there are a number of other ways that supremacy can present itself. As we have already explored, *fascism* in its own way is very much built upon the supremacy of one cultural group over all others and as we have already discussed, the sad annihilation of millions of Jews during the Second World War was built very much upon the idea of an Aryan superiority over the non-white, the non-blonde and the non-blue-eyed master race (Stanley, 2018).

Whilst it is not possible to explore ever single aspect of this table, there are a good number that it is worth considering in this book at this stage. *Thingification* is perhaps one of the most misunderstood means in which supremacy presents itself and actually allows us to begin to wedge open the door to understanding supremacy as a factor which sits outside of ourselves and edges us towards understanding supremacy as something which has a psychological context as well. Thingification is a term initially used by Aimé Césaire (2000) in his book where he explored the ability of the colonisers to not just obtain slaves for their own benefit but to dehumanise the slave to such an extent that they were nothing more than an object. The slave lost not only their name, but they also lost any sense of their history, any sense of their past, any sense of their knowledge, and their worth. They were denied the ability to read and to write. They were more often kept in such a system of ignorance that they were often seen by their oppressors as being less than human and therefore less deserving of respect than say their colonisers themselves.

Thingification through a racial lens is just one way this has presented itself. Thingification has ties also to the objectification of women; for example, the ongoing horrific idea within patriarchal environments that Incels cells believe they have a right to the bodies and the services of women based upon their own patriarchal position of superiority. This positioning of women as the other denies the humanity and the reality of said women and places them into a position where they are nothing more than objects for men to use (Casciani & De Simone, 2021).

What I am saying in both these instances so far is that white supremacy in its positioning of one group as superior to another, requires the Thingification of said other. Following this, patriarchy in its positioning of men as superior and dominant in its oppression of women, also involves the Thingification of the woman so much so that her humanity is lost and her ability to self-actualise is denied to her. These aspects of things that are not just rooted in past generations, they are very much a factor in the world that we live in today and play an enormous role in how we treat the other when we engage with our internal supremacist. We see the other and often ourselves as less than human. We see the other, and often ourselves, as unworthy of the same treatment which we would give out to others closest to us.

Thingification also occurs within a class system. The idea that one class is better than another and that the working classes do not deserve the same rights as those of the middle and upper classes, is something which in years gone by saw the rise of unions who often fought for the rights that they felt they deserved within a capitalist system. As per the previous story about Sylvia Pankhurst, this is something that she recognised, that her privilege gave her a responsibility to fight a superior system so that the working classes had better working environments, felt safe, their children were not used as labour and that sufficient time was given off for leave and sickness. In these fights for class rights, the class other therefore strives to have its humanity recognised and in that striving it meets resistance from the capitalist supremacy (M. King, 2015).

Another way that this perhaps occurs is in the level of support given to the disadvantaged and the working classes in cultures whereby discussions around social welfare, or the NHS in this country for example, are rife. To say more, the National Health Service was implemented in 1948 after the Second World War, a health service which has benefited millions of people in the United Kingdom ever since. The invention of a health service that was not necessarily free, but where one paid contributions in order to achieve and to obtain a level of health and substance that raised one's own humanity, in many ways was seen as an easy decision for a country that valued its population. This though has often run counter to the political ideologies of those from the right wing of this country, whereby ideas about a National Health Service then remove the Thingification of the lower classes and bring up the responsibility of the middle and upper classes for their lower-class kin. That the right will often reject said responsibility is a massive factor in the stripping back of the National Health Service by the current Conservative Government in order to capitalise upon its value, the view being to sell off such a national institution to the highest bidder somewhere else abroad.

This is just one example whereby care for the disadvantaged classes is pitched as a socialist ideology. Whereas what it really is in these instances is a recognition of the morality and the humanity inherent in the relationship between the upper classes and their working-class kin. Within counselling and psychotherapy Class-Thingification has also led to the increasing absence of numerous working class and disadvantaged students, often of colour or other forms of otherness, from trainings because of their inability to obtain funding to attend certain said courses. There is an ongoing failure of courses in not recognising that they have a moral obligation to create pathways and then to promote them within those harder to reach communities. This would then provide these same communities with a route towards training and therefore also a route back towards providing an invaluable service towards their own same communities. This failing is not just of psychotherapy institutions and trainings, not just of the profession, but shows a direct link between the capitalist need to make money within these services and the avoidance of responsibility for the other.

Thingification is not a new phrase. It is something that Martin Luther King has in the fight for civil rights and is a term that could also be applied to how we view the planet. As previously stated, we tend not to see ourselves as in a relationship to the world around us. We tend to see ourselves as separate to and therefore superior to the wider environment and yet, as Sir David Attenborough (2021) states in one of his many quotes on the topic area, it is this inability to recognise our own human position alongside the natural other that has led to the ravaging and destruction of natural resources which are finite and will run out in the near future. Thingification is an enormous factor therefore in how we see ourselves in relation to the world and to each other around us.

Moving on to the next layer of the diagram listed as Figure 2.1, what we see here is that there are two lines. It needs to be clearly stated that at present I see this section in between as being fluid in the fact that the line of con-sciousness and unconsciousness may move upwards of downwards dependent on the person, institution or system that is expressing these types of forms of oppression. Issues around ableism or ageism may not be far from the surface, meaning they often sit above that unconscious line and are very much in the world around us.

To return to exploring some of these facets, and these ideas as to how supremacy occurs, *heteronormativity* could be seen as a form of patriarchal supremacy whereby ideas about what it is to be a man is very much governed by those who are white, male and in particular heterosexual. This though has a cost and is a cost that has been widely reported and written about in the form of say toxic masculinity, whereby ideas about what it is to be a man marginalises and rejects anything that is seen as weak or is not manly enough. The consequence for those men who do not fit into such a narrow confine as a heteronormative heterosexual view of masculinity means that often certain men find themselves repressing aspects of their identity which might be seen as weak or as the other (Haider, 2016). As previously discussed, the rates of suicide in young men are a testimony to just how painful and difficult an experience this is for men in the Global North. Heteronormativity on the more political sphere has led to the marginalisation of the LGBTQ com-munity to the extent that it was only in the 1960s that homosexuality was decriminalised in the United Kingdom (Various, 2017).

Conversely, successive Conservative governments have also, in their shift to the political right, led to the marginalisation of the LGBTQ communities in this country. The impact of this has included between 1983 and 2003 a Conservative government policy which included Section 28, and the banning of the promotion of homosexuality in schools. A policy which led to the incitement of hatred towards the LGBTQ communities in the United Kingdom, meant that a heteronormative idea of identity was often that which would be promoted highest of all (Various, 2021e).

Heteronormativity as a form of patriarchal supremacy also has an impact on women. The heteronormative idea of what it is to be a woman in many ways has conversely led to the repression of certain aspects of identity that women hold and has also led to their own sort of homophobia against lesbian groups and so on. Finally, it should also be noted that heteronormativity has at its core, a religious idealism which underpins much of the supremacist ideas of patriarchy.

All of these examples sadly segway into a consideration of just how *Male Entitlement* plays a role in my ideas around supremacy. Male entitlement, as per the previously mentioned Incel movement believes that the rise of feminism amongst many other forms of equality has led to the oppression of certain types of men and that these men need to fight back to regain their position of control and supremacy. This shift is also replicated though in ideas around *Class Entitlement*, with class entitlement having close ties to the system of capitalism. What I mean by class entitlement in this instance is that those of the working classes believe that their rights are being impinged upon by minorities from outside of the country. For example, this is something we saw with the Brexit debate of 2016, a vote in which 52 per cent of the United Kingdom voted to remove itself from the Economic Union. Often on the basis of a number of stories, or I should say lies, whereby what was projected was a fear that minorities would march to this country in a wave or a flood that would overwhelm the resources here in the United Kingdom (Khomami, 2016; Stone, 2016). It is a method which has also been used politically in the United States where the Republican Party in their winning of the 2016 election, were able to tap into the disgruntled and silenced voices of an American working class that felt that its needs were not being met and that migrants, coming in this time from Mexico and South America, were the enemy there to steal, rape, and plunder (Yan et al., 2016). Class entitlement at its peak builds upon an idea of a fantasy of equality (in this case economic equality) and is something which is often projected towards the class other as a means of keeping them under control and enticing them into compliance.

Fascism is another form of supremacy and is a fairly easy one to explore and underline with numerous books having been written about the rise of fascism in Germany and across Europe before and during the Second World War. What is often less recognised is that this movement, this march towards an ideal of racial supremacy is something in which even the United Kingdom and the United States has found a foothold from the black shirts of 80 years ago to the march of far-right Nationalists onto the Capitol buildings in Washington DC in 2021 (Various, 2021f).

Racism is an area discussed in a good number of books on anti-racism, but to cover it here briefly the binary creation of race with race being something that those who see themselves as white have created to view themselves in relation to an against means that a fear and hatred of a racial other will also be apparent (Hall, 1997; Hudis, 2015). This places racism in the camp of supremacy because as this is a socially constructed idea, and clearly denotes that one race must be better than the other; that races are not created equal. For example, in quoting Biewen's (2017) work about the construction of race in his podcasts on Scene on Radio, the idea that there was always a hierarchy of race was posited which included the measuring of black skulls and the assessment of the behaviours of slaves who when they resisted slavery were designated to be mentally unwell. Racism works as well in the political sphere where different cultures and different races are measured against a white, European, often upper class or middle class ideal against which they can never be seen to be equal; against which there is always a hierarchical difference (Colin & Lund, n.d.).

It is also the same for *Sexism* where, as De Beauvoir (2010) stated in her work, the social construct of woman was something that was designed by men to identify themselves against. That in both instances persons of different races and women have often identified with this idea about how they should be in relation to whiteness and the patriarchy, shows the power of the intersectional supremacist ideal that sits within both of these isms. It also needs to be noted that both racism and sexism have also had religious perspectives interwoven into their fabric to such an extent that say persons of colour were deemed to be not acting within their God-given position should they resist and rebel against slavery, or that the rules of what it was to be a woman was often reinforced by the religious shaming of the church should they fail in their perceived duties (Akbar, 1984). The INCEL movement, just to briefly return to this group, has bought very much into these ideas and in some ways is an attempt to return culture to back to an idealised cast that never really was (an idea that I will discuss further on his chapter).

When we get to issues like *Classism* though, this follows on in the same vein. The easiest example that perhaps I could come up with is the fascination of those of across the Global North in the classist stereotypes presented in numerous programmes such as Upstairs Downstairs (Fellows, 2010), The Queen (Frears, 2016), and Downton Abbey (Fellows, 2010). That all of these programmes highlight the class split and how detached both classes are from each other, is underlined by the often-condescending relationship between those of a perceived higher class towards others of lower stature. Class is often used here as a way of making the lower-class other conform to way of being that is not of their own but is in service to the higher supreme position of the upper class or the middle class.

This social construction of class, like many of these others in this chapter, still exists today. That there are numerous immigrant workers in the United Kingdom working as anything from nannies to fruit pickers for middle class farmers and families is actually an unspoken, yet fairly common, aspect of our culture. The idea that the migrant other must know its place in service to the middle and upper classes fuels a work force in positions as diverse as from the National Health Service, to transport services, to cleaners and workers in office buildings, and so on, be it here in the United Kingdom or in other major cities within the Global North.

Classism plays a massive role within our training courses as well, whereby although it is readily noted that most of the psychotherapists in the United Kingdom, for example, are white and female. What is often less stated is that they are from a middle-class background. The intersection of their ability to actually fund said courses, together with having the time and the support to do so, means that it is often those of means in the United Kingdom who are able to access and take part in the two-to-four-year trainings that are offered within counselling and psychotherapy in the United Kingdom. Where this will be different to say the United States and across Europe is that most of these countries require anyone training to become a psychotherapist to have a First degree before doing so. This, therefore, leads to another layer of exclusion in that often times those who can afford to undertake said courses are again from those who are either able to fund it themselves or through family, but also the few who have been able to win some sort of scholarship or funding in order to compete at a level they might not have been able to achieve without such a route opening up before them (Adams, 2016).

To consider one or two more from the list: *Homophobia* and *Gay/Transphobia* again tie themselves to heteronormative ways of seeing identity, but also with the patriarchal idea of marginalising that which is seen as different. For example, Stonewall have stats which state 'One in five LGBT people (21 per cent) have experienced a hate crime or incident due to their sexual orientation and/or gender identity in the last 12 months', whilst 'Two in five trans people (41 per cent) have experienced a hate crime or incident because of their gender identity in the last 12 months and one in six LGB people, who aren't trans (16 per cent), have experienced a hate crime or incident due to their sexual orientation in the same period' (Bachmann & Gooch, 2017, p. 6). Incidents of hate against the LGBTQ community are very much driven by the patriarchal supremacy ideology that there is a way to be a heterosexual man and woman, and that anything that breaks this binary splitting, which plunges this ideal into the immense grey areas of identity orientation, must be resisted if not destroyed.

Ageism and *Ableism* could be tied to either capitalism as a form of oppression or the patriarchy. What I mean by making this statement is for somebody who is seen through an age-related bracket, it may well be that their use in a capitalist society is seen to have died away once they have reached a certain age whereby they are therefore deemed to be of no more use or value within a culture that continues to want to make money for itself. This is also apparent for an ableist perspective on the world. Simple things like accessibility to places, to theatres, cinemas, courses, universities, these are arenas which have often been built around an able-bodied person's require-ments therefore leading to the exclusion of those who are seen as differently able (Blytheway, 1995; Goodley, 2014).

Within the worlds of counselling and psychotherapy, many of our courses are quite ableist in their approach to the material being taught. A recent example presented on the Therapists Connect Podcast, where Victoria Nelson (Blundell, 2020) raised the idea that in a group setting where students were doing some personal development work, that a student with a hearing impairment found it incredibly difficult to relate to her peers in said group because she was unable to read all of the lips of those people speaking at any moment in time. It took the student herself to ask for a redesign of the group space to one whereby she was able to sit on the ground and change the angle, so that the group then became more inclusive for her. This was something which she should not have had to do were her different ability considered from the beginning of the course.

It is important to recognise how much we walk in an arena whereby because of the socially constructed nature of certain identities, supremacy rotates around us and within our world all the time. In my own practice, in my own work as a lecturer, even I have been challenged to look at where my own isms and obias might have pushed somebody to one side inadvertently or otherwise. My own experience in working with a deaf student was that over two periods of our work together, the first time I worked with her I did not know anything about her, I did not ask, I chose not to enquire, I remained cloaked in my ignorance. That this student felt it important to sit close to me I just put down to some sort of need for attachment to a strong male figure; reverting back if you like to a stereotypical and yet not totally illogical developmental reason for the student's need to be so close, but also my slight discomfort at her proximity. It was several years later, when said student pulled me to one side and said, 'We're going to be working together in the next couple of weeks and there is something that I need to say. I need you to know that I have a hearing impairment and under my hair I am wearing my hearing aids'. Whilst I was pleased that she had told me, and whilst I now understood the reasons for this student's need to tell me what she needed from me, I was also disappointed in myself that I had not been brave enough to create a safe enough space for said student to explore this material several years before.

What I am trying to show you in this chapter though, and in particular this section, is just how wide ranging and how intersectional some of these types of oppression actually are. That there are so many, that this is all very complicated, again shows the systemic ingrained enormous nature of supremacy. Yet, it is also important to recognise that whilst we may not be able to strip these aspects down one by one by recognising that they exist, we then give ourselves a chance to not only explore but to change our behaviours in relation to them.

The next section, though brings us more into the unconscious world of supremacy, aspects that I believe may well be under our radar but may still play themselves out accordingly.

Unconscious Supremacy

As we move this conversation into the world of the unconscious, the reason for this demarcation line is to state my position that many of the aspects of supremacy that we will be discussing from here onwards are more often than not unconscious. It is hugely important therefore to recognise some of these within us and within our clients, our practices, our institutions and our systems in order that we may better understand and if necessary, challenge and dismantle them accordingly.

The drive to *Elitism* is one which, although placed in the sort of unconscious space of this diagram of supremacy, is actually one which has a huge resonance in cultures across the Global North. That we have a class system which valorises the middle and upper classes as being seen as better than, more intelligent than, more special than and therefore better able to lead in many fashions, is a form of elitism that is both placed on a pedestal and at the same time valorised and aspired towards. In this country, elite institutions such as Eton have led to a disproportionate number of prime ministers and leaders of industry in this country (Duffell, 2014). This is no different to many of the countries in the Global North and it is a form of specialness which has led to persons from the colonies sending their children to elite schools here in the United Kingdom, in America and across Europe. One of my earliest statements in Chapter 1 holds elements of this elitist thinking of my parents in their decision to send myself to a school which would give me the best chance, not just to gain qualifications but to gain a foot up on the ladder towards a prominent position in industry.

This coincides though with *Class Sympathy, White Sympathy* and also *Himpathy*. When I use the phrase '+pathy', what I am stating clearly here is that as well as the valorisation of those seen as more prominent, more special, and more powerful, what the working classes, people of colour and women also do, is to offer additional sympathy for the 'plight' of those in the highest echelons in our societies no matter what misdemeanours they perform against us both through their gender, race or through their class. Himpathy is a term which was originally coined by Manne (2018) and spoke towards the idea that abusive, white heterosexual, wealthy men, when they are forced to face their sins of the past, are often given additional sympathy by not only other men but women as well because of their position in society and in culture.

This unconscious sympathy towards the abuser is something which sits in the world of class sympathy and also white sympathy as well, whereby the abuses of the patriarchal, white supremacist, capitalist triumvirate are minimised because they are seen to be in service to some kind of greater good, and whereby the morality necessary to challenge some of these systems has been removed or ignored. +pathy is therefore a quite powerful and insidious means for supremacy to retain its prominence and can also be generated through the supposed pseudo-vulnerability of perpetrators when they are placed upon the plinth in front of a judge or jury. Perfect examples of this are emerging from the faux emotional performances of the likes of Kyle Rittenhaus and Brett Kavanaugh and many other usually white, often heterosexual, always men (Sheets et al., 2021). The 'stratosphication of himpathy' is also afforded to the likes of Donald Trump who, even though millions if not billions around the world recognised his racism and heard the tapes about his sexism and his abuse of women, still chose to follow this man on social media and vote for him in the elections in the United States of America (Bobo, 2017; R. J. Diangelo, 2006).

White sympathy is an obvious facet of this argument. This was seen in the Capitol riots on 6 January 2021, whereby six people died in riots perpetrated by the far right and motivated most probably by the former President of the United States and some of his advisors (Various, 2021f). That these riots occurred at a time of racial tension in America is well documented, as is the fact that when Black Lives Matter protests took placed in the same city, the military were very much put on standby yet there was no riot. Yet, during the riots on 6 January that actually took place, the same level of security was nowhere to be seen, leading to the sad deaths of many and the injuring and fear of many, many more, not just in America but across the world.

White supremacy does not work, therefore, without a layer of sympathy gifted to it by those who desire its services. The same way that with a patriarchal system, while there are many people who challenge its supremacy, it does not exist without the complicity of a good number more who gain from the prominence that they have gathered under its auspices. This is also no different to within the world of class, where there will be those of the working classes who, in their efforts and aspirations to achieve a higher standard and position in society, will gladly pay sympathy towards those higher up the echelons whilst standing on the shoulders and the heads of those of a similar stratification.

Perhaps the most obvious metaphorical example of racial sympathy was emergent during the days of slavery where, in the splitting of a racialised culture between house, slave and field slave, oftentimes the house slaves, and in particular those who were charged with running said household, felt a certain kinship and sympathy towards their slave owner and their overseers. In the film Django Unchained, for example, Samuel L Jackson's character in on particular scene is seen crying uncontrollably after his master, played by Leonardo DiCaprio, has been shot and dies, even though he himself is nothing more than a slave who could be hung at any moment for any sort of crime (K. Andrews, 2016).

Moving to other areas of consideration, in a similar fashion to the sympathy gifted to those who hold supremacy, another way that supremacy recreates itself is to aspects such as *Mansplaining* and *Whitesplaining*. Mansplaining, as denoted by Dular (2021) is a term often used when women who are often very knowledgeable in whichever field or arena they work or exist within, find their material, their work, or their ideas explained back at them by a man. This effort to explain, control, and dominate the work of a woman is actually a micro-aggressive means that unconscious supremacist within certain men is activated and acts out. In the recognising that their position as superior at that particular moment does not exist and that they are in some way lesser to the gendered other, the fear of such a position, the fear that their ideal position has been sacrificed or lost, is so much for that unconscious ego to bear, that it finds and taps into its own sense of pseudo-knowledge and speaks up uncontrollably.

This is similar to whitesplaining; a term which I have borrowed and which is also called in some circles klansplaining (Godlee, 2021; V. E. Johnson et al., 2021). This involves the idea that there can be no person of colour who will know something more than somebody who is white. In the dream from the very first chapter, and the scenario presented there, as already stated the efforts of somebody who was white and female and their attempts to klansplain my own work back at me, is nothing new. One of the most interesting considerations I have found when writing articles or recording podcasts, was the number of always white, more often than not women, who felt the need to express that I was doing it wrong and that my work should follow a different route. Whilst their opinion is only that, an opinion, the interesting aspect is not so much the need to have and express said opinion, it is often the vitriol which sits behind it and the constant desire to reinforce that opinion in numerous messages, dia-tribes, or questions.

This is no different when it comes to our training courses. Often, one of the reasons why students who are minorities find it difficult to have a voice is because of the unconscious contract which leads to the silencing lest when they speak up; meaning they have their own opinions explained back at them, pathologised or shut down. To offer an example, though, of where the -splaining and the -impathy can sometimes collide: in my own work with a female client some ten years ago now, this came up in a very interesting fashion:

> The client, who I will call Kay, had been referred to me quite suddenly. Her previous therapist had apparently had to finish working with her within a week and the client had no idea as to why. Obviously upset, this client needed somebody to work with for a period of time, so she could process some of the feelings left over from what she experienced as a form of rejection. In our work together, though, what became apparent was that the client had taken a dislike to myself and to my methods and practice, stating on one occasion that she was concerned that I was even a therapist. Her reasoning was that occasionally just one or two slipped through the

net whilst on their trainings, and that I must have been one of those. The client did her six sessions and then calmly left, having received what help she needed through the attacks and the processing and having the chance to walk away in a way that she had not with her previous therapist. The denouement of the story though came to me in a message passed to me which stated that the previous therapist, a white male, had had to leave his practice because he had lost his licence to practice following some acting out with a female client. Kay had never asked the therapist what had happened and actually in a way, what I had received in the therapy was the rage and the anger at the inappropriateness of the previous therapist that she had not consciously felt able to express or been able to deliver within her previous therapy.

This is one of the reasons why I say the -splaining and the -impathy are actually unconscious. It is not to say that I am a perfect therapist. It is not to say that I always get everything right. But it is to say that this client is some way knew what was going on with the previous therapy and in particular the previous therapist. In a collusion of '+pathy', and without recognising the unconscious supremacy apparent, had stayed with this therapist for a number of years and only felt comfortable enough to show her rage towards that which she deemed to be less than her, in this case her new black, male psychotherapist.

The next areas to consider when looking at unconscious supremacy are the twinship of *historical erasure* and the *mythical past or traditionalism*. On Newsnight, a political panel show on the BBC, Laurence Fox on national television, pointed out that for him woke culture had gone too far because in the film 1917, as directed by Sam Mendez, there was a Sikh soldier presented as having fought during the First World War (Harrison, 2020). This was something which was echoed and repeated on social media, in letters to the BBC, and so on. The idea being that films like this should not re-write history in order to include persons of difference, be they women, or of colour, or of the LGBTQ community, therefore changing the 'true' historical narrative. The reality was that actually there were over one million Indian soldiers who served during the First World War, and a great many of these would have been Sikhs. Alongside this, there were many thousands more from the other colonies who travelled to Europe to take part in what was really a struggle between the British Empire and Germany.

Historical erasure in service to patriarchal and white supremacy ideals is a very insidious way of controlling the narrative and promoting the ideology that one is better than the racialised, gendered, or cultural other. The fact that so many failed to recognise that historical erasure has already happened, and that what they are being taught is only part of the story, therefore leads one to assume that this is another means by which white patriarchal society controls those within. In conjunction with this, another way that this works is through the projected narrative of a traditional ideal from many years past. A constant tool used within politics, the idea being that we should return to a time before the immigrants, a time before women worked, a time before whatever it is this week on the front of far-right newspapers. This idea creates a fantasy narrative that plays into the narcissism of the reader or the observer, so much so that they crave to make that fantasy a reality (Boffey, 2018).

The problem with this, though, is that whilst it never was and it never will be a reality, the fantasy that is being sold to one will often be found out to be a lie and a falsehood. The Brexit debate is a perfect example of traditionalising politics and selling a false narrative. It is actually an act involving the sanitisation of history. To return back to a time of a four-day week, rubbish on the streets, people living in council houses in Central London not long after the Second World War, then denies the fact that actually those were times which were very difficult, not just for minorities but for all of us across the country. This is not just a whitening of history, this is not just a patriarch-ing of history, this is the most brilliant salesmanship of an idealised history that if we all buy into actually increases the wealth and standing of a few over the many.

Moving on to several other areas to consider from the chart, *imposter syndrome* and *inferiority complex* are both incredibly important when we come to understanding issues of supremacy. Imposter syndrome involves the idea that one does not measure up to the ideals of others, that one has been lucky in order to gain a position of influence or importance within an organisation (Bothello & Roulet, 2019; Wilkinson, 2020).

This is something with which I can personally resonate. Back in 2007, when I first undertook a lecture of any kind in the world of academia, I remember being both frightened, surprised, and honoured that I had been given said chance. Not feeling worthy of the position though, led me to under prepare and feel incredibly intimidated by those who had asked me to give a presentation, as well as those I was presenting towards. In this particular incident, the students I was working with were white, male and female and of a comparable age to myself. I was the only person of colour, as usual, in the room. In some ways, the racial difference is only of marginal importance and what resonates a lot more is the idea that as an outsider, and as a minority, I did not feel that I had the right, the experience, the knowledge, or the talent, to be sat in front of these people offering a lecture. Said lecture, if I am brutally honest, went appalling badly, so much so that the colleague who asked me to do the presentation gave me a minor telling off for my lack of preparation, my nerves and my sense of inferiority. That telling off though, in a personal way, actually led me to challenge myself to become the best presenter I could be, be it within academia or at conferences.

Now, the reason I am telling this particular story is in the hope that for many others, in particular for women, the sense that one is an imposter when seen through the story of somebody similar, will resonate. Imposter syndrome suggests though an internalised unconscious comparison with the subject; it speaks of a belief that one is not only not good enough, but also that one is not worthy and that this belief can never be changed. What goes with this though is the sense that imposter syndrome and an inferiority complex are really deeply ingrained within patriarchal, capitalist and racialised narratives about who is able to hold the position that one has been offered. It is something that afflicts men of the majorities in power far less than it does those of a different class, race, gender, or creed.

As we walk down this hierarchy though, what we increasingly see is the more nuanced ways that the comparisons with the triumvirate at the top engender deep within us all. *Microaggressions* though sits within this wheelhouse as well. Often, microaggressions are pitched as 'It was just a joke', but what often happens with these forms of aggressions is that there is an attempt by the subject to both put down and silence the other in whichever form. One is told that one has a chip on their shoulder, that we are too sensitive, that we are being hysterical or that they are acting out to use a psychotherapeutic phrase, normally after an experience where the subject has unleashed something upon the other which is both offensive and detrimental to their mental health. The psychological impact of a microaggression in the splitting of the other between what they know has happened to them versus the part that believes that the subject is true to their word and means them no harm, suggests microaggressions have a deepening impact upon the other.

To offer an example, in a paper written for Therapy Today in 2021 (D. Turner, 2021), I utilised a number of quotes from letters that I had received telling me off for not bringing people together and for creating racial division. In one of these incidents though, the perpetrator then subsequently sent me a second message to say that they still loved me, and I would still be their friend. Microaggressions like this often have a double strand attached. There is the strand of offence and there is a strand of pseudo-reparation, where no apology is apparent and where blame for the impact of the statement or the action is pushed towards the other. The impact of microaggressions has been explored a lot in recent years in the work of Cousins and Barry (2021), where everything from racialised, genderised, or other forms of micro-aggressive behaviour is considered, together with how to survive said experiences through techniques or ways of expressing oneself is presented.

Where microaggressions though tie themselves together with say another aspect of unconscious supremacy, which is *silencing,* is that in the aggressive act the other is not supposed to have a voice and in the presentation of a pseudo-apology there is a silencing of the anger and frustration and the pain of the act endured by the other. I have written in the past about how these acts are actually ways that the subject rids itself of aspects of its identity it does not wish to hold and I have considered how microaggressions are a part of the projected identification bridge which ties subject and other together (D. D. L. Turner, 2021).

What should also be added here though is that these forms of abuses of the other have their roots within the systemic supremacy of patriarchy, white supremacy and capitalism and are often used against many groups which sit outside of the higher echelons of the triumvirate. These could be from the highest echelons of government, where major politicians have quite often told their female colleagues to 'Calm down dear' or have told them to check their tongue when speaking to a 'superior' man. That *tone policing* is also on this list, is an extension of the micro-aggressive supremacist and even should the other be watching their tongue, what is often loaded into the statement to watch one's tongue is the idea that 'you do not speak to me this way, I am superior to you, I therefore will be obeyed'. Terms like this have often been used historically in cultures like this one, for example during the Victorian age, where the tone and the position of women was monitored and managed by men in power so that they were not to be seen as too aggressive, too challenging in their voice or in their mannerisms. Or should they ever glance up and stare a man in the eye, that was often seen as a form of challenge towards the patriarchal superiority of said father, husband or other author-itarian (Moore, 2010). Tone policing is therefore not just about the voice, it is about the manner and the mannerisms of the other as designated and denoted by those in power.

As we approach the bottom of this table, the areas of consideration here are no less important that some of the others in the unconscious space, in fact they carry just as much weight as some of the others. For example, using the use of *ableist* or *ageist* language is something which quite obviously excludes and marginalises those who are deemed to be older or who have been seen as less comparably able to those who are young or able bodied. This is not just about the obvious ways that one might be seen as able, it may also involve using language which silences those with less visible disabilities, such as those which are more neurological (Aosved et al., 2009; Blytheway, 1995; Goodley, 2014; Wolbring, 2012).

Deadnaming is another one which is quite important to recognise and is the continued use, often against transgendered individuals and groups, of names long since silenced by those by the non-binary other in the LGBTQ com-munity. Tying this one together with the form of a microaggression is not too far of a stretch as the pain caused by the re-awakening of a dead name in its usage against the other can run deep psychologically (Earnshaw et al., 2020; Turton, 2021). Names from a cultural and racial perspective are also mas-sively important. Using the story of a gentleman called Simon, his parents had come to the United Kingdom from Vietnam when he was a child and was one of the many families who fled the country at the end of the Vietnam war. On arrival to this country, his family gave up their name in order to better fit in with British culture. Simon though found this quite distressing as he grew older and, in our work, he recognised that his original name tied him back to his culture and cultural background and that destruction of said name meant in some ways the destruction of that part of himself which marked him out as Vietnamese. Our work therefore involved Simon attempting to return to his roots through casting off, or the death of, his Westernised name and re-incorporating that which he had been forced to put to one side by his well-meaning parents. That certain members of his family and some of his friends refused to accept this, became a massive attack upon Simon's identity.

I am very aware in presenting this issue here in this book that I am choosing to use a Westernised name for this client. Yet, given the need to make confidential said material, and asking the client which name he would choose to use, this was the name that he preferred as it was one that he named his own child by.

Summary

This chapter has looked at how systemic, institutional, and individual supremacy actually appears in our world. The idea that supremacy is just about whiteness is hugely flawed and incredibly reductionistic and does not recognise that when there are socially constructed ideas of identity, and that these social constructions come with them a hierarchy of who is better or worse than the other. Authors from De Beauvoir to Judith Butler have explored this narrative ad infinitum, the hierarchical nature of social constructs and it is an area of concern for our trainings as counsellor and psy-chotherapists that we struggle to see these things play themselves out, not just in the world but in our courses, amongst our students, within our teaching faculties and within our client cases and therapy rooms (Butler, 1997; Sartre & Kaufmann Mccall, 1979).

What this chapter has also done is show how ingrained and rooted many of these behaviours are within our Westernised society. Supremacy is therefore not just a singular thing, but is that which we are all immersed within, be us the other or of privilege. In fact, one way of escaping the pain of being othered is by building that internal and external hierarchy and making somebody else feel less than ourselves; by engaging with our own internalised supremacist.

The next chapter though will start to explore how psychotherapy and its own perspective and ideas might assist in understanding the ways in which supremacy forms, how it is maintained and its deeper psychological impact. This is why this next chapter, like this book is called *The Psychology of Supremacy*.

References

Adams, R. (2016, September). Third of students at many British boarding schools come from overseas. *Guardian Online*, 1–2.

Ahmed, S. (2007). A phenomenology of whiteness. *Feminist Theory*, 8(2), 149–168. 10.1177/1464700107078139

Akbar, N. (1984). *Breaking the Chains of Psychological Slavery.* New Mind.

Alim, N. (2010). Therapeutic progressions of client and therapist throughout a course of psychodynamic therapy with a man with mild learning disabilities and anger problems. *Advances in Mental Health and Learning Disabilities, 4*(1), 42–48. 10.5 042/amhld.2010.0058

Andersen, P. D. (2014). The Hollywood beach party genre and the exotification of youthful white masculinity in early 1960s America. *Men and Masculinities, 18*(5), 511–535. 10.1177/1097184×14558880

Andrews, K. (2016). The psychosis of whiteness: the celluloid hallucinations of amazing Graze and Belle. *Journal of Black Studies,* 1–13. 10.1177/002193471663 8802

Andrews, T. (2012). What is social constructionism? *The Grounded Theory Review, 11*(1), 39–46.

Aosved, A. C., Long, P. J., & Voller, E. K. (2009). Measuring sexism, racism, sexual prejudice, ageism, classism, and religious intolerance: the intolerant schema measure. *Journal of Applied Social Psychology, 39*(10), 2321–2354. 10.1111/j.1559-181 6.2009.00528.x

Attenborough, D. (2021). COP26: not fear, but hope. *COP26, 1.* https://www.bbc.co. uk/news/av/science-environment-59121615

Bachmann, C. L., & Gooch, B. (2017). *LGBT in Britain: Hate Crime and Discrimination.* https://www.stonewall.org.uk/lgbt-britain-hate-crime-and-discrimination

Baldwin, J. (2017). *I'm Not Your Negro.* Penguin Classics.

Bannerji, H. (2000). The paradox of diversity: the construction of a multicultural Canada and "women of color." *Women's Studies International Forum, 23*(5), 537–560. 10.1227/01.NEU.0000028086.48597.4F

Barnes, E. (2016). *The Minority Body: A Theory of Disability.* OUP.

Beauvoir, S. de. (2010). *The Second Sex.* Alfred A. Knopf.

Bettcher, T. M. (2014). Trapped in the wrong theory: rethinking trans oppression and resistance. *Source: Signs, 39*(2), 383–406. 10.1086/673088

Biewen, J. (2017). *Seeing White (Part 2 How race was made?).* Scene on Radio. https://www.acast.com/cdspodcas/how-race-was-made-seeing-white-part-2

Biewen, J., & Headlee, C. (2018). *Men (Series 3): Dick Move.* Scene on Radio. http:// www.sceneonradio.org/episode-47-dick-move-men-part-1/

Blundell, P. (2020). *Therapists Connect Podcast. Episode 10 – Victoria Nelson.* Apple Podcasts. https://podcasts.apple.com/gb/podcast/episode-10-victoria-nelson/ id1518054312?i=1000488517850

Blytheway, B. (1995). *Ageism.* Open University Press.

Bobo, L. D. (2017). Racism in Trump's America: reflections on culture, sociology, and the 2016 US presidential election. *British Journal of Sociology, 68*(November), S85–S104. 10.1111/1468-4446.12324

Boffey, D. (2018, November). Empire 2.0: the fantasy that's fuelling Tory divisions on Brexit. *Guardian Online, 1.* https://www.theguardian.com/politics/2018/nov/08/ empire-fantasy-fuelling-tory-divisions-on-brexit

Bothello, J., & Roulet, T. J. (2019). The imposter syndrome, or the mis-representation of self in academic life. *Journal of Management Studies, 56*(4), 854–861. 10.1111/ joms.12344

British Psychological Society. (2020). *DCP Racial and Social Inequalities in the Times of Covid-19 Working Group.*

Butler, J. (1990). *Gender Trouble.* Routledge.

Butler, J. (1997). Merely cultural. *Social Text, 52/53,* 265. 10.2307/466744

Casciani, D., & De Simone, D. (2021). *Incels: A New Terror Threat to the UK?* BBC News Online. https://www.bbc.co.uk/news/uk-58207064

Cesaire, A. (2000). *Discourse on Colonialism.* Monthly Review Press.

Cesarino, L. (2012). Brazilian post-coloniality and south-south cooperation: a view from anthropology. *Portuguese Cultural Studies, 4*(Fall 2012), 85–113.

Cheung, M., & Nguyen, P. V. (2012). Connecting the strengths of Gestalt chairs to Asian clients. *Smith College Studies in Social Work, 82*(1), 51–62. 10.1080/00377317.2012.638895

Cianconi, P., Betrò, S., & Janiri, L. (2020). The impact of climate change on mental health: a systematic descriptive review. *Frontiers in Psychiatry, 11*(March), 1–15. 10.3389/fpsyt.2020.00074

Colin, S. A. J., & Lund, C. L. (n.d.). *The Intersections of White Privilege and Racism: Moving Forward.* 10.1002/ace.365

Collins, P. H. (2019). *Intersectionality as Critical Social Theory.* Duke University Press.

Commission on Race and Ethnic Disparities. (2021). *Commission on Race and Ethnic Disparities: The Report* (Issue March). https://assets.publishing.service.gov.uk/government/uploads/system/uploads/attachment_data/file/974507/20210331_-_CRED_Report_-_FINAL_-_Web_Accessible.pdf

Cousins, S., & Diamond, B. (2021). *Making Sense of Microaggressions.* Open Voices.

DeGruy, J. (2005). *Post Traumatic Slave Syndrome: America's Legacy of Enduring Injury and Healing.* Joy Degruy Publications.

Diangelo, R. (2018). *White Fragility: Why It's So Hard for White People to Talk about Racism.* Beacon Press.

Diangelo, R. J. (2006). My class didn't trump my race: using oppression to face privilege. *Multiulrural Perspectives, 8*(1), 51–56. 10.1207/s15327892mcp0801_9org/10.1207/s15327892mcp0801_9

Dudley, M. Q. (2017). A library matter of genocide: the library of congress and the historiography of the Native American Holocaust. *International Indigenous Policy Journal, 8*(2). 10.18584/iipj.2017.8.2.9

Duffell, N. (2014, June). G2: why boarding schools make bad leaders: the elite tradition is to send children away at a young age to be educated. But future politicians who suffer this' privileged abandonment' often turn out as bullies or bumblers. *The Guardian, 10,* 1–5.

Dular, N. (2021). Mansplaining as epistemic injustice. *Feminist Philosophy Quarterly, 7*(1). 10.5206/fpq/2021.1.8482

Durant, S. (Ed.). (1994). *The War of the Words: The Political Correctness Debate.* Virago.

Earnshaw, V. A., Menino, D. D., Sava, L. M., Perrotti, J., Barnes, T. N., Humphrey, D. L., & Reisner, S. L. (2020). LGBTQ bullying: a qualitative investigation of student and school health professional perspectives. *Journal of LGBT Youth, 17*(3), 280–297. 10.1080/19361653.2019.1653808

Fanon, F. (2005). *Black Skin, White Mask* (M. Silverman (Ed.)). Manchester University Press.

Fellows, J. (2010). *Downton Abbey*. ITV. https://www.itv.com/presscentre/ep1week30/downton-abbey

Frears, S. (2016). *The Queen*. Netflix. https://www.netflix.com/pn/title/70052705

Godlee, F. (2021). Speaking truth to power. *The BMJ, 372*, 95–98. 10.1136/bmj.n24

Goodley, D. (2014). *Dis/ability Studies: Theorising Disablism and Ableism*. Routledge.

Haider, S. (2016). The shooting in Orlando, terrorism or toxic masculinity (or both?). *Men and Masculinities, 19*(5), 555–565. 10.1177/1097184×16664952

Hall, S. (1997). Who needs identity. *The British Journal of Sociology, 48*(1), 208. 10.23 07/591920

Hancock, C. (2013). Invisible others: Muslims in European cities in the time of the burqa ban. *Treballs de La Societat Catalana de Geografia, 75*, 135–148. https://doi.org/10.2436/20.3002.01.25

Harris, S. R. (2006). Social constructionism and social inequality: an introduction to a special issue of JCE. *Journal of Contemporary Ethnography, 35*(3), 223–235. 10.11 77/0891241606286816

Harrison, E. (2020). *Laurence Fox Accuses Woman of Racism for Calling Him a 'White Privileged Male' in Question Time Clash*. Independent Online. https://www.independent.co.uk/arts-entertainment/tv/news/laurence-fox-meghan-markle-question-time-racism-bbc-video-a9287971.html

Hawkes, S. (2020). The banality of the patriarchy. *The Lancet, 396*(10263), 1624–1625. 10.1016/s0140-6736(20)32416-8

Heejung, C. (2020). How to stop lockdown reinforcing old-school gender roles. *Western Mail*, 1–3. https://search.proquest.com/newspapers/how-stop-lockdown-reinforcing-old-

Hegel, G. (1976). *Phenomenology of Spirit*. Oxford University Press.

Hudis, P. (2015). Frantz Fanon's contribution to Hegelian Marxism. *Critical Sociology*, 1–9. 10.1177/0896920515610894

Independent Review of the Mental Health Act. (2018). *Modernising the Mental Health Act – Summary Version*. December.

IPCC. (2021). IPCC press release AR6. *Climate Change 2013 – The Physical Science Basis*, August 2021, 1–6.

Jackson, C., & Turner, D. (2021). The big interview. *Therapy Today*, May.

Jacobs, M. (2003). *Sigmund Freud – Key Figures in Counselling and Psychotherapy* (2nd ed.). SAGE Publications.

Johnson, R. A. (1986). *Inner Work: Using Dreams and Active Imagination for Personal Growth*. Harper San Francisco.

Johnson, V. E., Nadal, K. L., Sissoko, D. R. G., & King, R. (2021). "It's not in your head": gaslighting, 'splaining, victim blaming, and other harmful reactions to microaggressions. *Perspectives on Psychological Science, 16*(5), 1024–1036. 10.1177/1 7456916211011963

Jung, C. G. (1963). *Mysterium Coniuntionis* (2nd ed.). Princeton University Press.

Jung, C. G. (1997). *Jung on Active Imagination* (J. Chodorow (Ed.)). Routledge.

Kapp, S. K., Gillespie-Lynch, K., Sherman, L. E., & Hutman, T. (n.d.). *Developmental Psychology Deficit, Difference, or Both? Autism and Neurodiversity Deficit, Difference, or Both? Autism and Neurodiversity*. 10.1037/a0028353

Khomami, N. (2016). The vote made people just explode: polish centre reeling after graffiti attack. *The Guardian*. www.theguardian.com/uk-news/2016/jun/27/brexit-polish-centre-london-reeling-after-graffiti-attack

King, H. S., & Ghost, L. S. (2011). The Holocaust as a paradigm for the Congo atrocities: Adam Hochschild's "King Leopold's Ghost." *Criticism, 53*(4), 587–606. https://www.jstor.org/stable/23133898

King, M. (2015). The "knockout game": moral panic and the politics of white victimhood. *Race Relations, 56*(4), 85–94. 10.1177/0306396814567411

Kingsford-Smith, A. (2014). *Disguised in Dance: The Secret History of Capoeira*. Brazil: The Best of Its Art and Culture. http://theculturetrip.com/south-america/brazil/articles/disguised-in-dance-the-secret-history-of-capoeira/

Lev Kenaan, V. (2021). Digging with Freud: from hysteria to the birth of a new philology. *American Imago, 78*(2), 341–366. 10.1353/AIM.2021.0015

Lorde, A. (1984). *Sister Outsider*. Crossing Press Limited.

Manne, K. (2018). Brett Kavanaugh and America's 'Himpathy' reckoning. *The New York Times*, 1–3. https://www.nytimes.com/2018/09/26/opinion/brett-kavanaugh-hearing-himpathy.html

Maurer, R. (2012). The power of the empty chair. *The Journal for Quality and Participation, July*, 10–12. http://www.asq.org/pub/jqp

Merrick, R., & White, N. (2021). *United Nations experts condemn 'shocking' race report and call for commission to be scrapped*. Independent Online. https://www.independent.co.uk/news/uk/politics/race-report-un-boris-johnson-commission-b1833671.html

Mintz, K. (2017). Ableism, ambiguity, and the Anna Stubblefield case. *Disability and Society, 32*(10), 1666–1670. 10.1080/09687599.2017.1356058

Moore, G. (2010). Imperial white: race, diaspora and the British Empire/enacting Englishness in the Victorian period: colonialism and the politics of performance. *Journal of Victorian Culture, 15*(3), 409–413. 10.1080/13555502.2010.519548

Morton, B. (2021). *Sarah Everard: how Wayne Couzens planned her murder*. BBC News Online. https://www.bbc.co.uk/news/uk-58746108

Neimeyer, R. a. (1998). Social constructionism in the counselling context. *Counselling Psychology Quarterly, 11*(2), 135–149. 10.1080/09515079808254050

Office for National Statistics. (2014). Suicides in England, 2013. In *2014*. https://media.samaritans.org/documents/Suicide_Stats_England_2020_FINAL_eONhYYF.pdf

Ohito, E. O. (2019). "I just love black people!": love, pleasure, and critical pedagogy in urban teacher education. *Urban Review, 51*(1), 123–145. 10.1007/s11256-018-0492-7

Oxford Languages. (2012). *Oxford English Dictionary*. Oxford University Press.

Pankhurst, R. (1979). *Sylvia Pankhurst: Artist and Crusader*. Paddington Press.

Pereira, J. L. (2016). The Roman Catholic Church and Slavery in José Evaristo d'Almeida's O Escravo (The Slave). *Dialog, 55*(3), 239–246. 10.1111/dial.12260

Potts, M., & Campbell, M. (2008). The origins and future of patriarchy: the biological background of gender politics. *Journal of Family Planning and Reproductive Health Care, 34*(3), 171–174. 10.1783/147118908784734792

Prados-Ojeda, J. L., Gordillo-Urbano, R. M., Carrillo-Pérez, T., Vázquez-Calvo, A., Herrera-Cortés, M. A., Carreño-Ruiz, M. Á., & Font-Ugalde, P. (2021). Suicide presentations to an emergency department pre and during the COVID lockdown, March-May 2020, in Spain. *Archives of Suicide Research: Official Journal of the*

International Academy for Suicide Research, *0*(0), 1–13. 10.1080/13811118.2021. 1887023

Procter, J. (2004). Encoding/decoding. In *Stuart Hall*. 10.1080/09502380500077730

Proctor, J. (2004). *Stuart Hall: Routledge Critical Thinkers*. Routledge.

Pugh, M. (2008). *The Pankhursts: The History of One Radical Family*. Vintage Books.

Richardson, J. S. (1991). Imperium Romanum: empire and the language of power author. *The Journal of Roman Studies*, *81*(1991), 1–9.

Richardson, L., Beadle-Brown, J., Bradshaw, J., Guest, C., Malovic, A., & Himmerich, J. (2016). "I felt that I deserved it" – experiences and implications of disability hate crime. *Tizard Learning Disability Review*, *21*(2), 80–88. 10.1108/ TLDR-03-2015-0010

Rousseau, J.-J. (1998). *The Social Contract*. Wordsworth Editions Limited.

Sánchez, F. J., & Vilain, E. (2012). "Straight-acting gays": the relationship between masculine consciousness, anti-effeminacy, and negative gay identity. *Archives of Sexual Behavior*, *41*(1), 111–119. 10.1007/s10508-012-9912-z

Sartre, J.-P., & Kaufmann Mccall, D. (1979). Simone de Beauvoir, "the second sex" Simone de Beauvoir, the second sex, and Jean-Paul Sartre. *Source: Signs*, *5*(2), 209–223.

Schubert, M. (n.d.). *The "German nation" and the "black other": social Darwinism and the cultural mission in German colonial discourse*. 10.1080/0031322X.2011.624754

Sheets, M., Vallejo, J., Sly, E., Massie, G., Woodward, A., Hirwani, P., & Bancroft, H. (2021). *Kyle Rittenhouse verdict: gun group to 'award' AR-15 to teen as defence attorney calls Trump Jr 'idiot'*. Independent Online. https://www.independent.co.uk/news/world/ americas/crime/kyle-rittenhouse-shooting-verdict-victims-b1961611.html

Singh, N. (2021). *Biden calls White Supremacists "demented"*. The Independent. https://www.msn.com/en-gb/news/world/biden-calls-white-supremacists-demented/ ar-BB1dL3VU

Spivak, G. C. (1988). Can the subaltern speak? In *Marxism and the Interpretation of Culture* (pp. 271–312). 10.1590/S0102-44501999000200012

Stanley, J. (2018). *How Fascism Works: The Politics of Us and Them*. Random House.

Stone, J. (2016). *EU referendum: Baroness Warsi subjected to Islamophobic abuse by Brexit supporters after defecting*. Independent Online. http://www.independent.co. uk/news/uk/politics/eu-referendum-baroness-warsi-defect-islamophobic-abuse-brexit-supporters-remain-leave-a7091076.html

Summers, H. (2021). *Black women in the UK four times more likely to die in pregnancy or childbirth*. Guardian Online. https://www.theguardian.com/global-development/ 2021/jan/15/black-women-in-the-uk-four-times-more-likely-to-die-in-pregnancy-or-childbirth

Sydney, U. of T. (2020). *Hoarding and herding during the Covid-19 pandemic*. Science Daily. https://www.sciencedaily.com/releases/2020/09/200910100608.htm

Thomas, L. K. (2000). Attachment Issues between a Caribbean Mother and Daughter. *Separation & Reunion Forum and Goldsmiths College Joint Conference, June 2000*, 1–27. http://files/623/Thomas - Unknown - Attachment Issues Between a Caribbean Mother and Daughter.pdf

Turner, D. (2016a). Examining Buber's I: narcissism and the othering of the other. *Journal of Critical Psychology Counselling and Psychotherapy*, *16*(June), 113–117.

Turner, D. (2016b). Born again: an alchemical exploration of the dreams of the other. *IASD*, *45*, 1–8.

Turner, D. (2021). Why we still need black history month. *Therapy Today*, October, 2012.

Turner, D. D. L. (2021). *Intersections of Privilege and Otherness in Counselling and Psychotherapy* (1st ed.). Routledge.

Turton, S. (2021). Deadnaming as disformative utterance: the redefinition of trans womanhood on Urban Dictionary. *Gender and Language*, *15*(1), 42–64. 10.1558/genl.18816

Unknown (2020). *Rule, Britannia! Will be sun on last night of the proms after BBC U-turn.* BBC News Online. https://www.bbc.co.uk/news/entertainment-arts-53998584#:~:text= The BBC has reversed its decision not to, dropped due to associations with colonialism and slavery.

Unknown (2021). *Canada: 751 unmarked graves found at residential school.* BBC News Online. https://www.bbc.co.uk/news/world-us-canada-57592243

Various (2000). Text of the White House statements on the human genome project. *The New York Times*. https://archive.nytimes.com/www.nytimes.com/library/national/science/062700sci-genome-text.html

Various (2017). A timeline of gay rights in the UK. *The Week*. https://www.theweek.co.uk/87213/a-timeline-of-gay-rights-in-the-uk

Various (2019a). Discrimination in mental health services. *Mind*. https://www.mind.org.uk/news-campaigns/legal-news/legal-newsletter-june-2019/discrimination-in-mental-health-services/

Various (2019b). *Removal of indigenous children is a human rights concern.* Australian Human Rights Commission. https://humanrights.gov.au/about/news/removal-indigenous-children-human-rights-concern

Various (2020). *George Floyd Death.* BBC News. https://www.bbc.co.uk/news/topics/cv7wlylxzg1t/george-floyd-death

Various (2021a). *Defaced Marcus Rashford Mural covered in supportive notes.* BBC News. https://www.bbc.co.uk/news/uk-england-manchester-57806142

Various (2021b). *Ethnicity facts and figures: stop and search statistics.* GOV.UK. https://www.ethnicity-facts-figures.service.gov.uk/crime-justice-and-the-law/policing/stop-and-search/latest#by-ethnicity

Various (2021c). *Female soctor who robs boys of role models, claims Tory MP.* BBC News Online. https://www.bbc.co.uk/news/uk-politics-59421259

Various (2021d). *Has George Floyd changed Britain?* ITV. https://www.itv.com/presscentre/ep1week19/trevor-mcdonald-charlene-white-has-george-floyd-changed-britain#

Various (2021e). *Schools and colleges.* Stonewall. https://www.stonewall.org.uk/schools-colleges#:~:text=Stonewall was founded on 24 May 1989%2 C one,a total suppression of LGBTQ%2B identities in schools.

Various (2021f). U.S. Capitol riot. *The New York Times*. https://www.nytimes.com/spotlight/us-capitol-riots-investigations

von Franz, M.-L. (1980). *Projection and Re-Collection in Jungian Psychology.* Open Court Publications.

Wigger, I. (2010). 'Black Shame' – the campaign against 'racial degeneration' and female degradation in interwar Europe. *Race Relations*, *51*(3), 33–46. 10.1177/0306396809354444

Wilkinson, C. (2020). Imposter syndrome and the accidental academic: an auto-ethnographic account. *International Journal for Academic Development, 25*(4), 363–374. 10.1080/1360144X.2020.1762087

Wolbring, G. (2012). Expanding Ableism: taking down the Ghettoization of impact of disability studies scholars. *Societies, 2*, 75–83. 10.3390/soc2030075

Yan, H., Ellis, R., & Rogers, K. (2016). *Reports of racist graffiti, hate crimes in Trump's America.* CNN. http://edition.cnn.com/2016/11/10/us/post-election-hate-crimes-and-fears-trnd/

Chapter 3

The Psychology of Supremacy

Whilst the two previous chapters have presented an overview and exploration of how supremacy sits within our culture, this chapter begins a psychotherapeutic exploration of just how supremacy is formed and maintained. As I have already stated in the earlier two chapters, given the social construction of identity that we all are engaged within or formed by, we all have certain aspects of our psyche which form build a hierarchy of one part over another; we all hold an internalised supremacist.

This process though, of recognising where supremacy sits within each of us, begins at a very early age. Children do not marginalise and discriminate based around the protective characteristics of the 2010 Equality Act here in the UK for example or around any other legislation from the US and other countries (Government, 2010). This is one of the reasons why in schools, the drives towards equality and recognition of difference are slightly flawed in their makeup. Whilst it is positive for our educational establishments to recognise and celebrate difference and to encourage our children to do the same, it is also imperative for them to recognise that difference and otherness and in particular the prejudices that they will form and hold, are an important and essential aspect of them building a sense of who they are. It is essential to recognise not only this, but also the role of parents, care givers, teachers, culture, religions, and other organisations and systems and their influence upon said children.

To offer you an example of what I am talking about here, it is worth exploring the work of Jean Piaget. Piaget was a Swiss psychologist who was born in 1896. A close contemporary of Sigmund Freud, he did a lot of work in understanding the role of prejudice in child development (Weil & Piaget, 1951). In a similar vein to some of the ideas expressed by Sigmund Freud, and their recognition of the influence of the culture of the time (including the rise of Nazism), Piaget recognised that children go through some very specific stages in understanding who they are in relation to the other. His work in mapping these stages finding space alongside the work of theorists such as Melanie Kline and John Bowlby (Bowlby, 1988; Mitchell, 1986).

To better explore some of these stages, Piaget recognised that between the ages between zero and two are when a baby is very much unaware of the

DOI: 10.4324/9781003313229-3

individuality of its parents or care givers around itself. It is very much the centre of a world, the centre of a group, a family, a culture, and its ability to recognise the other, whilst there, is limited in that it believes that at best what it can do is mimic the behaviours of another and internalise said experiences.

This is hugely important; that mimicry of the behaviours of others literally starts the day a child is born. A story from my own history illuminates this quite well, about the day my daughter was born. In the months previous to her birth, I was attending parenting classes with my then wife. During one of these sessions, I was told that were I to stick my tongue out in the minutes after my child was born that said child would reciprocate. Feeling this was a bit silly, I chose not to believe this. Sadly, my then wife had a difficult birth so when my daughter was finally delivered by Caesarean, I was asked to hold her and nurture my young daughter through the first few minutes of her new life. At some point, it occurred to me that I should try the simple act of getting this child to mimic me and looking my daughter in her eye, I stuck my tongue out. My minutes old daughter of course did the same. The consequence of this particularly simple example was one of this author's heart melting and his falling instantly in love with said child. Whilst this example is not about difference, and it is not about supremacy, what it does show is the power of a parent; the power of a care giver to influence and impact upon a child. A power that begins mere minutes after birth.

The mimicry displayed here is something which many of us use in adult life (Brighi & Cerella, 2015; Ram, 2014). From the urge to code-switch, where persons of difference change anything from their tone of voice and language, to their clothes, to their habits, when in majority spaces, code-switching involves a form of mimicry of the majority environments (Leonardo, 2004). Mimicry could also involve playing up to an ideal laid out to oneself based around one's gender or ability. In some ways we all perform, we all mimic ways of being. Yet, for many the issue with mimicry in later life is that this can lead to the sense of inauthenticity which can lead to psychological and occasional physical traumas (Fredrickson & Harrison, 2005; Williams et al., 2022).

Moving slightly further forward, between the ages of two and six, for Jean Piaget, the child starts to develop an egocentric sense of self. They are able to express what they mean, and they are aware of the other, but that awareness is tempered as they are unable to assume the perspective of or to empathise with said other. At this point, I would like to bring in the ideas of Frances Aboud, who in her work considered this stage between two and six as being hugely important (Aboud, 1988). Here she breaks down this stage into two particular distinct sub-stages. For her, between the ages of three and four, a child is able to start to understand the difference between them and another and understand the explanations given to them by said adults. An example of this arose from some work I did with a client whereby she and her three-year-old boy were walking down the road one spring afternoon. Whilst meandering down the street, a Muslim woman walks past wearing a hijab. The boy looks up at this woman, having not seen someone in a hijab before, and he points and makes the sort of comment that a three-year-old would make. The mother though laughs (an action both out of her own embarrassment and her own prejudice). What it does lead to is the mimicking behaviour we have just discussed as her three-year-old son decides to join in with the laughter and keeps on pointing. What we start to see here is not necessarily a racialised expression of something from the child, but the parent's fear and ignorance of difference then being played out and normalised through the child.

This is why I suggest that it is hugely important that the role of the groups around us, and the systems that we inhabit are essential when it comes to adjusting or changing issues of prejudice and racism, homophobia, etc that propagate our cultures. Whilst it starts with children, and whilst children are a blank slate, often it is the unresolved issues of the parents which create added discord within the psyches of said children. This is where prejudices start to form for children. This idea of who they are and who another is involves them putting down the other in the form of a micro or a more overt form of prejudice.

Between the ages of five and six though for Aboud, children can better understand and internalise the experiences and the knowledge of their parents and of others around them. They are also able to make distinctions between not only the externalised groups outside of themselves, but also members of their own racial, gender, or other types of groups.

Between the ages of seven and eight, Piaget felt that a child should be able to move from a more egocentric perspective to one which is more sociocentric. This is where empathy starts to come in, whereby instead of just performing the role of another, as a child will do anyway, what they are able to do is assume the perspective and the emotional landscape of another. They are able to understand the other that sits across from them (Weil & Piaget, 1951).

Aboud though took this a stage even further, recognising that at this particular point, children can better understand and express some of the difficult feelings that there are around their own gender group, sexual orientation, racial or cultural identity or disability, be it pride or of sadness and shame (Aboud, 1993).

This brief overview and understanding of the developmental nature of difference also filter into the world of supremacy. What I should add here, is that both Piaget's and Aboud's work explored the social constructs of identity in children. What they also do, inadvertently I suspect, is explore the hierarchical nature of these same constructs. Children form a sense of who they are and who they are not, not necessarily just to separate themselves out from one another, but also to denote who is superior in the group, them or another. My idea here shifts Piaget and Aboud's ideas fundamentally in that it started to recognise that as well as there being a subject and object, the subject is one above the other.

This is vastly different from a more biological exploration of differences, whereby actually what is there are two parts set alongside each other, A and B, subject-object, self and other. When we factor in the idea of identity formation and the fear and internalised impressions of said family culture, gender, or whatever it might be, what we also end up with is a third entity. Figure 3.1 below speaks about this succinctly.

To speak to this briefly before I offer an example, what we have here is three different elements; an external superego which is often informed by those who care for us and therefore holds sway and dominance over an egoic sense of self that we formed accordingly. What this means is we are built from the experiences of our parents and their experiences of their own social constructionist identities, as they are built from their parents and the social construction of their identities and so on. In order for us to maintain that egoic sense of self though, there has got to be an other to marginalise, to denigrate, to put down. This is the third entity. This is why the superego and the ego often work together and shows why there needs to be an other which therefore binds the superego and ego in unity.

Whilst this might seem slightly complex, I want to offer a simple example from my own history, which will hopefully explain what I actually mean by this. When my daughter was three years of age, she was at nursery one summer. She had been going there for about a year, she was very well settled, and she had a good number of friends. Given that I live near the coast, as often happens families would come down from London and deposit their children in local nurseries whilst they, the parents, went off for days out to do their own thing.

One particular summer's day, a six-year-old child had turned up at the nursery and had not long after arriving decided that she would dictate the

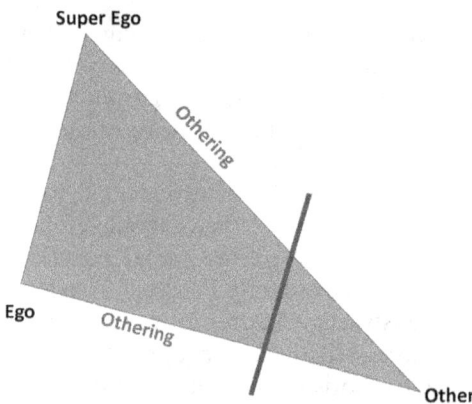

Figure 3.1 The Psychological Creation of the Other.

games that the children would play, children of varying ages between three and five. In doing so, what she chose to do was to marginalise my daughter. When my daughter asked her why this was, the girl of six years of age told my daughter that it was because her skin was ugly, and her hair was dirty. Nobody would play with my daughter on that particular day. My daughter came home understandably upset and in tears and believing that she was ugly based on her skin and on her hair. When challenged though, the nursery took the party line stating that they always include every child and that they have a zero-tolerance policy to issues of prejudice, racism, and marginalisation. As I have stated here though, what they failed to recognise were a couple of things: There was a six-year-old child who had been left in a nursery whose identity is suddenly challenged by the presence of not just a whole lot of new people, but somebody of colour as well. The second aspect was that the six-year-old child was obviously terrified, and in trying to find her footing in such a new space she defined who was in her group and who was the other. The messages she gave out to my daughter were not necessarily those that were constructed from her own narrative, but were also those that she would have imbibed from her own familial and cultural experiences, etc.

To close off the story of my daughter, recognising for myself the importance of care for young girls of colour, myself and my daughter watched a lovely film called Hair Love which won an Oscar in 2019 (Cherry et al., 2019). On the back of watching that film and recognising the institutional and systemic nature of the external and internalised hatred of black girls' hair, my daughter and I took it upon ourselves to challenge said views. We then constructed a ritual whereby each Sunday that she is with me we would do her hair; I would wash her hair, she would dry it and I would style it with her as we watched a film on television. The influence of me as her parent is therefore there to counteract the influence of the six-year-old on my daughter but also the influence of said six-year-old's parents on the six-year-old and especially upon my daughter.

Returning to Figure 3.1, the reason I expressed this story is because the superego in these instances was the parents of the six-year-old. These superego parents were responsible for the internalised messages that were passed on to the six-year-old. They influenced the fragile egoic sense of self of the six-year-old, an ego which was challenged by being in a new environment where she knew nobody, an ego held together by forming a group around herself, and the simultaneous creation of the other. That other, on this occasion, was my daughter.

Although this is presented through an early life lens, it should be noted that these experiences are often used in other arenas as well. One of the more common ones is emergent when a political elite uses their position to manipulate its voting population, often made up of the working classes, by creating an other to hate and to be fearful of. In the 2016 election of Donald Trump, his ability to speak to the silent voices of the blue-collar workers in the US and his success in this instance, was built very much upon the ability to create a Mexican other to hate (Bobo, 2017). Be it immigrants climbing over the wall that he pledged to build; be it minorities already residing in the States whose votes needed to be taken away because they were deemed not to be American enough; or be it the press and the media, this projection of the victimhood of the blue collared worker was built upon an other by a cultural superego in the form of an elite.

To take this into a little bit more detail, what the six-year-old had done in a way was to re-emphasise the racial identity of her parents and her culture by stating categorically in that interaction what she was and what she is not. She was the other children who were mainly white in that nursery, she was not the young three-year-old black girl. The interesting thing about his example is the non-recognition of the impact of othering. Here othering is the non-realisation that a person is more than just one or two fixed identities and that they are a multitude of identities that all jostle together at any given moment in time. Also, instead they focus on aspects of identity which reduce the opposite person accordingly in this case hair and skin (Kirschner, 2012).

Othering for children is actually a fairly common factor and, whilst it should not be stamped out, it should be considered for what it actually is, which is an aspect of identity formation. Children though marginalise for a wide variety of reasons; the other could be too large, too small, too tall, too thin, they may say something silly at some point, or they may be too intelligent. Children play this part out in order for them to feel safe but often at the expense of another person. It is this expense which needs to be weighed up and considered when enacting or putting in place systems and procedures to help children recognise the impact they are having on others.

Although the examples given thus far speak predominantly of how children form identity and how this identity is built upon socially constructed prejudices, that is not to say that this does not occur for adults as well. Presenting my client Frankie, his story here brings this early formation of identity into the therapy room and starts to show how this might occur for adults as well as children. When Frankie entered my therapy room, he was 28 years of age, suffering from depression, loneliness, and existential anxiety. He wanted to understand not just how his early life had impacted his sense of who he was as an adult, but also how to manage these feelings, in particular his feelings of sadness and loneliness. Frankie's father was a prominent businessman having built up his own business empire over a number of years in the East End of London. Frankie also had a brother who in this instance I shall call Mike. Their father was very much the head of the home, believing in traditional values and taking it upon himself to make all of the main decisions for the family. One such decision was to send them both to private schools in the East End of London. One of the things that Frankie experienced whilst at school was that even though he was the older brother to Mike, it was he who was often bullied and picked on at school. When he would complain to his father though, his father often denigrated him, putting him down and seeing him as not strong enough to actually cope with the tough environment of a school in the East End of London.

When I spoke to Frankie about this incident whereby, he had been critiqued by his own father and questioned what that must have been like for him, Frankie shrugged his shoulders. 'This was a regular occurrence for me', said Frankie. 'Because my father always preferred my brother, Mike over myself'. It was important for us to look at how in Frankie's world he was marked as an outsider, whereas his brother, Mike was measured as being included in the family unit and where the father's pride was often showered upon him to an extent that he could do no wrong. This left Frankie feeling as if conversely anything that he did or said or produced in terms of schoolwork would often be ignored or put down. This pattern of separation created a schism between himself and his brother, so much so that at the time of our work together they barely spoke to each other and the only time they ever saw each other, even though they lived in the same city, would be for a few hours on Christmas Day should they be at their father's home at the same time. Frankie often felt un-cared for by his father, unloved in fact, and even though he had a fairly decent job, lived with his girlfriend, and had an adequate circle of friends, according to him, there was always this underlying sense of sadness, pain, and isolation.

Much of what is in this story can be considered through varying psy-chological lenses, but because this book takes into account the world of supremacy, it is important for us to explore how the psychological side of supremacy, especially developmentally, can play a role in the psychological make up of our clients.

Our exploration of Frankie's world uncovered a few interesting truths. The first was the role of the patriarch; that of Frankie's father. As previously stated in Figure 3.1, what can often happen in creating and maintaining a socially con-structed system of superiority, is that there needs to be a superego that domi-nates an ego that then splits off and creates the other. In this instance, Frankie and Mike are the brothers split in two dominated by a father who, for whatever reason, had decided that his worth and his position as the patriarchal centre, nay pinnacle of his family unit, needed to be maintained. So, whereas the good father should be able to nurture both sons so that they are able to achieve their own roots in life, thereby moving beyond said father, the superior father conversely will look to maintain his own position of superiority by undermining in this instance Franke and also, I should add, Mike. From what little I knew of Mike, it seemed like although he was younger than Frankie and although he was very much revered and respected, seemingly by his own father, in his own way he had not begun to achieve in the world or live up to his full potential; this was a younger brother who in his mid-twenties partied a lot, smoked a lot of dope and was still borrowing money from his father ad infinitum.

The importance of the undermining nature of unconscious patriarchal supremacy is that in seeming to offer one son in this instance a position of prominence by creating an other in the form of a brother who could be scapegoated and dismissed, what actually happens is that the valued brother is as equally undermined and abused as the unvalued one. The snippets of treats, the unearned money, the allowance to do and perform in a way that was not afforded to Frankie, thereby becomes a means of subtle control whereby where neither brother is actually able to challenge or surpass the insecure supremacy of the patriarch.

There is one other element though that needs to be added to this narrative and that appears in the form of Figure 3.2 above which lays this out. Developing an idea suggested by Haug (2008) the feminist psychologist the idea here is that supremacy really is not about a pinnacle, it is not about who is at the top and who is at the bottom, what it really is about is who is at the centre. What maintaining this position also involves is an understanding of just how the central core manipulates those in its orbit as it attempts to maintain its narcissistic position of centrality.

Returning to Frankie's example then, he here is the other, that which sits on the outside, whilst the father is quite obviously at the central point. The outlier could be seen to be Mike. In that outlier position though, it should be noted that the outlier is far enough away from the central point so as not to challenge its worth, authority, and superiority. This does not mean that Frankie did not try to engage his father and move further inwards toward the centre. Yet, it was those moments which were most painful for him in that the father would often verbally abuse him, put him down, or keep repeating the same phrases over and over again as a means of wearing his own son down so his son gave up and relented. Those conversations, some of which

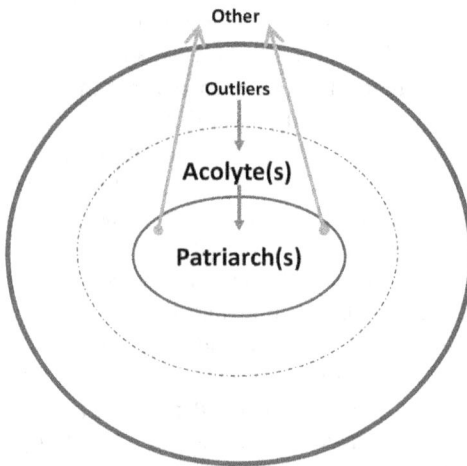

Figure 3.2 How Supremacy maintains itself.

were held over the phone, would often leave Frankie feeling so frustrated and angry that he would throw the phone down on his own father. On other occasions, the father would often tell him directly to his face that he was not his son, that he could not believe they came from the same stock, and they were nothing alike, things which hurt Frankie to his core.

There is one other factor here which has not been considered and that is the role of the acolyte. No system of centrality can ever exist without a rallying call to those who will rotate around central point and do its bidding. In Frankie's example, his mother played an important role in maintaining the father's position as superior, in that she often kept silent when the father said things which she may or may not have agreed with. She often enacted the wishes of the father, listening to her son, perhaps hearing his concerns but choosing to do nothing about them and it was she who would often also turn a blind eye to the unhealthy machinations of Mike, ways of being which often frustrated Frankie when he saw them continuing.

Acolytes here play a major role in maintaining the pinnacle position of the patriarch, the supremacist, or the capitalist. For example, in instances of Female Genital Mutilation, although this is often couched in religious patriarchy, it is often the role of the matriarchs of the community to carry out such a horrific practice (Berer, 2019). Systemically, this is important. Just like how in systemic family work persons within said family take up different positions in different roles, when we factor in the idea of supremacy, those roles take on a very different picture (Jakimowicz et al., 2021). It is important therefore to recognise that for an individual their constructed position in this instance is a familiar one defined within a socially constructed narrative of patriarchal supremacy.

Another way of seeing how supremacy is actually a part of all our psychologies is by remembering that Albert Adler hinted and walked towards such a presumption in his own work (Orgler, 1973; Way, 1956). His idea being that an inferiority complex was something generated within all of us as we formed a sense of who we are in the world, our identity, be it socially constructed or otherwise, being influenced by circumstances I have already mentioned, such as family and culture. He also posited the idea that in order to escape the sense of inferiority which we may all inhabit, we build a superior defence against any sense of feeling of lack imbued within an inferiority complex. This internalised sense of superiority gives rise to ideas of narcissistic perfection and self-idealisation that can appear within clients or students (Gordon & Dombeck, 2010; Zeigler-Hill et al., 2008). The sense that when faced with an other, who for example does not fit with the culturally generated ideas that one has been fed, one engages in a superior defence whereby we put down the therapist, the lecturer, we look for some sense of conflict within the therapeutic space in order to re-establish our internalised sense of superiority.

The example presented earlier in Chapter 2 of the client who criticised my work whilst also engaging in a process of himpathy and white sympathy, is an example of a superior defence activated within a white, middle class, hetero-sexual woman who had been taught that she was superior to the racialised other of the therapist. As I have stated previously, one of the reasons why persons of difference across the board often feel that they need to work twice as hard as the subject in order to achieve their goals or that they feel like imposters when out working in the world is because their internalised superior, as an aspect of the superego, has whispered in their ear that they are as such.

Some of the hints for how a superiority complex or a superior ego might occur are actually emergent in the ways that the ego tries to restore its superiority and the types of stereotypes that it will engage within in order to do so.

What I am saying here, is that when we factor in white supremacy in these narratives, when the superego, external or internal, and the ego no longer find that their axis keeps them away from the other, or when the other starts to speak up, what will happen is the supremacist axis between superego and ego will reveal its hate. This too will happen in courses. In these instances, fear and hatred are key. They are pivotal in understanding the fragile nature of the self-imposed egoic link between the super ego and the ego. Although this may hold echoes of Diangelo's (2018) work around white fragility, as I will re-state, whilst I agree in her suggestions, my sense is this concept that she has designed does not hold as much weight as it could do. My view here is that what is being threatened is a sense of superiority that runs to the core of every socially constructed egoic sense of self that we all hold in some way. So no different to the client who comes to therapy looking for therapy and then resists said therapy, the supremacist may wish to see their own racism but they resist seeing t. r own racism at exactly the same time. Yet, it is there. For the axis to therefore remain safe within its own ignorance, the other, which I should also add is a split-off part of said ego, must also remain silent. The other must not knock on the door of acknowledgement, it must sit safely ensconced in the unconscious from where it should not act out.

The Supremacy Complex

Complexes, as Jung states, are independent things of their own; they sit outside of our knowledge and challenge us momentarily, daily, weekly, monthly, and yearly. They attempt to bring the shadow into consciousness. In our counselling and psychotherapy courses, even the least experiential ones, we are always challenged to face our shadows. We are challenged every time we meet somebody, be they someone new, someone we know, or someone we were raised with. We are challenged to learn more about ourselves every minute, every day, every month, and every year. A defence against these sorts of interactions and how they might change us, in particular around the socially constructed aspects of our identities, is something I have titled the supremacy complex. To understand this, therefore, means considering how this particular complex plays a pivotal role in helping us defend against the changing tides of relationship, be they literal or psychological.

To offer another example of how superiority and inferiority and the other appear within our culture, one only has to look through the annals of European history to discover where this has occurred. An interesting example from British history could be around the Highland Clearances enacted between approximately 1750 and 1860 after the Battle of Culloden (Mackinnon, 2017; Valdés Miyares, 2017). The clearances involved the movement of huge swathes of people from their holdings in central Scotland towards the coast initially. This movement enacted under English rule paved the way for many of the gentrified land holdings that still exist in Scotland today. Persons who were then actually moved to the coastal areas and put to work to pay rent and bills to their mainly English landowners, were then often parcelled off and encouraged to leave Scotland completely and sent to the New World of America. Being paid to go was often cheaper for the English than it was for them to keep people on their land where they would pay bills subsequently.

One of the interesting parts about this whole story, when I factor in the supremacy complex and its external relevance, is that although we can see a split between the English as a cultural superego and the cleared Scots at the other, what we should also not is that there were often a good number of Scottish nationals who sided with the English. This split in a cultural psyche between pro-English and anti-English Scots is something which sits within the culture to this day; in fact, it was a major facet in how colonialism worked across the countries colonised by the Europeans. The script was often to take those who had been invaded or co-opted and split them in two. Pro and against. So, in a way what we see again is how the supremacy complex works within a colonised system whereby the only people who ultimately win is those with the power of the superego. Those who are their acolytes are often promised much more than they received and the other is left out in the cold or moved around accordingly.

The egoic or the cultural cost was often that there was a loss of identity for those of the cultural other, a sadness in particular played out in Scotland and perhaps resisted to some degree in Wales, whereby a similar process was undergone. In the 14th century, in Wales, the borough system was implemented by the Tudors leading to the near extinction of much of Welsh culture and the attempted annihilation of the rich Welsh language (Goodman, 970; Hodges, 2021; Jones, 1998). Colonialism works by a process of superiority but also utilises a system of cultural splitting in order to reinforce its ideas and ideals. Within that, though, there will always be resistance to making a true cultural identity illegal. This does not mean that true cultural identity totally dies, as the partly othered sense of self (in these cases language, cultural norms, and identity) does not disappear. What can happen is they lie dormant waiting for some generation further down the line to reclaim them, reinstitute them, and make them relevant again.

One of the most important things to explore in this triangulation between the superego, the ego, and the other is to start to recognise the role of a superego in this context. For everyone from Sigmund Freud onwards, the superego is very much there to direct and control the behaviours of said ego (Wurmser, 2015). It is very much informed by the cultural, societal, and gender norms of the time, the ideas here having strong connections to social constructionist ideas of identity. With my exploration, it is also worth exploring a little bit further just how strong the superego's role and position actually is, especially when we come to ideas of supremacy.

The superego manages its egoic counterpart. The ego needs said superego in order to self-identify and it looks to the superego for its guidance and identity formation. The superego conversely assists the ego recognising who it is by shaving off or creating an other, be it internally or externally that the ego can then reject. It should also be noted that the superego can be broken down into different types or aspects. These could be a cultural superego or a gender-based superego, or a superego which holds tight to an idea of one's sexual identity or one that recognises its position as a disabled other. The superego, therefore, has a huge role in mitigating the social constructionist aspect of the egoic forms under its auspices. To say a little bit more and to offer an example for the culturally superior aspect of the superego, in its defining of a cultural egoic sense of sense, what it will do is it will contrast this ego either with another culture which it deems to be other and therefore bad or wrong or foreign in some way, or it will work in the framework of defining of what it is to be culturally superior and thereby ridding one's egoic sense of self of aspects, behaviours, actions, ways of being which sit outside of that cultural norm.

These socially constructed aspects of the superego though hold very little feeling. They are disconnected from their own humanity having cast off their own sense of inferiority into the egoic sense of self which it dominates. The paradox within this though is that even within this type of super egoic othering, the humanity which is inherent within us all is still necessary, and the superego will therefore keep or attempt to keep the ego close to itself, denying said humanity and forcing it into the shadow.

This superior/inferior defence against the other is what therefore creates an internal and external barrier against difference. The ego idolises the superego, in particular in its absence, and projects onto it aspects of itself that it wishes to have, seeing them as special, particular or necessary in order to function as a better 'human' being, person, or group. Conversely, the superego promises the ego that it can be all of these things. It is like the snake whispering on the vine of the tree in the Garden of Eden saying that if one only committed these small and hugely significant acts in its name, one would then be allowed the riches promised by said snake (Various, 2016).

There is a sense, therefore, for the ego of always living within the world of a promise, within the world of hope, and this is where the positioning of an acolyte becomes most important. Acolytes by their very nature are driven by the idea that they will achieve the level of specialness afforded to the guru or the person at the top of the pyramid. In order to do so, they will perform whatever acts that superior personage or grouping decrees of them. These can be horrible acts or acts where one crosses one's own moral boundaries and yet for one driven purely by one's egoic sense of self, in this case, an acolyte, to not do so risks being cast out into the purgatory of otherness.

Factoring in the superego's supremacy in relation to issues of difference, otherness, and equality, when we return back to Figure 2.1 in Chapter 2, the superego works subtly and well to create a narrative whereby alternative visions or histories are annihilated. As we have already seen, the historical importance of minorities from many different groups is often expunged from our history books so that often we are left, in particular in academic spaces, with a history that is very much sanitised, very much white, male and middle class, and within the world of counselling and psychotherapy, often is quite old.

The one aspect of this that needs to be noted is the role of the other in this triage. The other here will often times play its role compliantly, silently, and without complaint. Yet when it chooses to do so, and I do use the word choice for a reason, then it does so from a position of unconsciousness, an unconsciousness driven into it through the oppressive stances of the superego and the ego or based upon decades if not hundreds of years of othering which has become internalised. Yet, when we talk about wokeness, what we actually mean is the self-actualising potential of the unconscious other has risen to the surface. To be woke on an individual level means that one's own unconscious split is starting to stir, that whatever we have been encouraged to lay to one side in order to fit into a culture of supremacy, has started to fall away because our adaptations fit us no longer. When the other starts to speak up, the threat is less so to the egoic sense of self which in turn will wake up but is more so to the super egoic sense of superiority whose power is then under threat.

As an example, during the Second World War, there were 200,000 troops that came from America to the United Kingdom pre-D-Day. One of the most cliched and popular narratives of the time was the fear of a lot of English men that Americans coming over to the United Kingdom would lead to them stealing their women and other such stereotypical ideas. On a very simplistic level, this is an encounter with otherness. The others in this instance being Americans coming across to serve within the allies. The patriarchal narrative of the time was one to protect the women who, in this case, will be seen as the egoic core. The importance of this should not be understated. In a patriarchal society that at that time dominated the role of women in society, to then have another group, in this case, Americans, come across, then led to a real cultural challenge for the English patriarchy. Their ideas about Americans would have been very much based around stereotypes and cliched ideas about what Americans were all about. Yet the reality when lots of Americans arrived in the United Kingdom was vastly different, the reality being one of relationship and co-operation on the whole, although of course there will always be instances whereby the stereotypes rang true.

Another example comes out of some work I performed with a client named Ernest. Ernest was a man in his fifties who had been raised in Birmingham in a mixed heritage family. His father had come from the Caribbean and had been in this country for a short period of time. His mother, who was English and working class, had met the father and they had a brief fling from which Ernest and one of his brothers were born. Not long after Ernest's younger brother arrived, the father suddenly left, returning to the Caribbean from where Ernest never saw him again, perhaps only receiving the occasional letter when his father felt it was time to get in contact. Ernest's mother, as I have said, was from a working-class background in Birmingham in the 1960s. Her family though were white, with there being no other children of colour in the immediate or extended family. Ernest had a good life within this family unit, he spent a lot of time with his cousins, he enjoyed school, and did well for himself, yet as he got older he realised that his experience of persons of colour was very much limited to the stereotypical ideas that he had been presented with when he was growing up.

In our work together, Ernest told me that for him black people were thieves, robbers, and other stereotypes. Yet, as an intelligent man, he realised that these were cliches but ideas that nonetheless frightened him to his core. Ernest was very much driven to try and understand and explore his own cultural identity, but within this drive to do so, saw the cultural other, in this case, his Caribbean background, as being something scary, something other. Our work, therefore, meant that we spent a lot of time with him sitting with a man of colour in a room de-constructing a good number of the stereotypes that he had been left with, so much so that he eventually decided to take a trip to the Caribbean, his first time away to meet members of his family from his father's side. One of the kindest and sweetest things about our work together was that when he left the therapy, after about a year, Ernest gave me the lovely gift of a book telling the story of Sidney Poitier's life. In some ways, this was a symbolic gesture for both of us. It was not just a gift for me but was also a recognition that his internalised cultural self had moved on from the stereotypical ideas of media and television of his youth to one whereby he was able to engage with symbols, metaphors, and idols that held something true to him, Ernest an experienced, successful black male, just like Sidney Poitier.

Symbols of Supremacy

In moving onward to the unconscious experience of supremacy, it is important to restate that the use of creativity has been a cornerstone of my work in these explorations around the social constructions of identity. The work of Dora Kalff and her ideas around sand play have proven to be essential here

(Kalff, 1991; Turner, 2005). With my use of sand play being utilised as a less intrusive means of understanding unconscious processes, recognising any exploration of said processes would need to involve a means by which the logical, cognitive mind was not so much supplanted, but was moved beyond (Cox & Thielgaard, 1986).

Sand play work follows a process which recognises that we all internalise experiences (Schaverien, 2005). As stated in Chapter 1, these socially constructed internalisations then move us and motivate us to be either who we are told to be by our family, our culture, our religion, and so on, and quite often involve us rejecting the instinctual drive to be more authentically ourselves. There are numerous theorists who have considered this split between a false self and its adaptations and a true self (Bowlby, 1973; Mitchell, 1986). This material has been explored since the earliest days of psychotherapy. What these theorists have failed to do until now, is to look at how the social constructions of identity filter into this internalisation of a false sense of self.

Alongside other such methods, such as active imagination, dreamwork, and other creative means, Sand play work offers one means of exploring this internalised unconscious landscape (Hamilton, 2014; Jung, 1997). The general process is such that when working with a client, or a participant in these instances, the person in the room was invited to use myself as a screen for their projected internalisations of supremacy. In order to reveal and then explore this projection, the participant was asked to select two symbols, one for themselves and one for myself as they saw me during our interview. These symbols were then placed out in a tray of sand and were followed by an oral exploration with myself as to their meaning and their positioning and what that might reflect on the nature of our relationship.

It is important to recognise that I have stayed within the confines of the understandings presented by my participants in this exercise and any additional layer of exploration has been laid over the top so as not to supplant the phenomenological experience of supremacy of said participant (Moustakas, 1994). The first example is presented below by Dianna.

For Dianna her difference was partly racial, with this aspect being that she identified as a black woman born in majority-white London. Her second intersectional difference is cultural, as when she was younger her parents took her to Africa where she struggled to fit in as she was considered European and therefore an outsider. When her mother brought the family back to the UK a couple of years later, her mother joined her local church which also left her feeling like an outsider as she was different from her friends. Dianna has also been drawn to differences throughout her life, which included having moved around Europe a fair amount with work and marrying an Italian man. She had three children.

For out sand play exercise, Dianna chose a Cat for herself seeing me as a turtle. When she placed these in the tray, as displayed in Figure 3.3, she

Figure 3.3 Dianna's Sand Tray.

placed the cat in the corner of the tray, with the turtle slowly moving towards it. We moved the symbols around from time to time and this generated the following discussion:

'Dianna:	well, you hesitated, I kind of sensed that you kind of almost … well I asked myself, do I put here, or do I put it there? I was very aware of where I put you, but I suppose I didn't have to worry as there was nothing else there, I just put mine in the corner, and I just, I was interested in why I put you facing that way, obviously directionally.
DT:	I think it's just the idea of travelling, I had an idea of it (the turtle) travelling across in some way.
Dianna:	but then you could also say it … because it's going slowly, and if that moved it would quicker.
DT:	that is a good point, notice how this feels when I do this. (Moves the turtle so it faces the cat) What does that bring up for you?
Dianna:	a bit more anxiety.

DT:	what is the anxiety about?
Dianna:	like I've been seen I suppose. And the sense of getting closer and there is really nowhere to go as I'm in the corner.
DT:	so now you feel trapped in the corner, and this person isn't moving fast by the way. So now you can't escape from there? I'm exaggerating this by the way. So actually, you felt safer this way when it was facing away.
Dianna:	Its funny you just do that. I can feel more relaxed when you do that. Yeah'.

For Dianna, the conflict between being seen as other and having control over what people see of her seemed to be alive for a lot of the time. Yet alongside this, Dianna's choice of an instinctual animal was quite telling. There was a power in this figure, but there was also a great deal of fear of the symbol she had chosen for me. This contrasted with the selection of the turtle, a symbol which could be seen as quite feminine and maternal, yet also held echoes of Dianna's upbringing, given she was raised predominantly by her own mother.

The racialised aspect of being a woman, and a black woman, who has to hide herself, is nothing new to women of colour. Being seen, or not being seen in this case, is something learned within the home from an early age, I will argue here. The power of white supremacy to marginalise, and invisibilise blackness, is a topic explored by many theorists (Kinouani, 2021; Lowe, 2008). In a similar vein to the destruction of cultural norms endured by the Celts within the British Isles by the English, making invisible that which is different is also a core tenet of the colonial project (Ram, 2014; Schubert, n.d.; Valdés Miyares, 2017). Even the ideas of the politics of assimilation, as pushed by the government of Margaret Thatcher in the 1980s, worked to make invisible that which was the racial other (Unknown, 2014). The impact of this upon women of colour, and its internalisation here in Dianna's sand tray, should therefore also not be underestimated.

The next highly interesting point involved Dianna's placement of her symbol in the corner of the tray. This struggle to take up a more prominent position, say for example in the centre of the tray, says a lot about the power dynamics that she has internalised from her own family unit. Whilst there are many ways of assessing Dianna's experiences, one means of consideration here is to look through the lenses of the triumvirate of patriarchy, white supremacy, and colonialism. Here the superego is the turtle and her egoic compliant sense of self is the kitten in the corner of the sand tray. Here, there is a major distancing of herself from her power, much like that presented in Figure 3.1 as well. This here is a literal playing out of the power system derived from Haug's (2008) work.

Moving forward to another example, this one involved a participant named Elsa. Although born and raised on the South Coast of England, for Elsa her experience of being an outsider began with witnessing her mother being bullied by the other mothers in her neighbourhood because she was Greek and seen as attractive. Raised with a number of illnesses like eczema and dyslexia and having to wear an eye patch, Elsa was often excluded by her peers at school. For Elsa, these early experiences of marginalisation because of her culture, her neurodiversity, and because of her skin condition, all of which coloured her life yet also meant that she was more daring than others in her adult life, as she had set up a business to help disadvantaged children.

As we explored the power dynamics unconsciously present in the interview, Elsa selected the symbol of Gilgamesh for herself, whereas she chose a Lego cowboy to represent myself as her interviewer. In discussing the two symbols Elsa said (Figure 3.4):

Figure 3.4 Elsa's Sand Tray.

'Elsa: *It looks like it's going to trample mine.*
DT: *Why have you put him up there?*
Elsa: *Because it looks like you're going to step on him*
DT: *Why is he going to step on him?*
Elsa: *Because he is a cowboy.*
DT: *Cowboys don't just step on things, do they?*
Elsa: *But he looks like he will run towards (him).*
DT: *He's stood still, he has got his hands out, so your fear is that …*
Elsa: *He doesn't feel right like that*
DT: *But even that is interesting*
Elsa: *I've got a massive fear that you're going to squish mine*
DT: *What is that fear about? There is a fear that my cowboy is going to squash Gilgamesh, is that right?*
Elsa: *I think so, it's obviously Hindu isn't it.*
DT: *(at this point I remove the Cowboy from the sand tray) So, if I do this and I move him from here and what happens?*
Elsa: *I feel really relaxed.*
DT: *Really?*
Elsa: *Yeah. Do you know what it reminds me of, it reminds me in a waiting room upstairs of when your own your own. Love it. The moment when people come in, I freak.*
DT: *Really? I notice you've just rubbed out his footprint. He's really got something over you.*
(Lots of laughing at this point)
DT: *I'm going to put him back. But notice that tension. Don't worry, he isn't coming for you. I assure you he will stay right there. But that fear is acute.*
Elsa: *It is really, it is uncomfortable.*
DT: *So much so that he has to be removed?*
Elsa: *I could literally put him out there.*
DT: *Move him down there.*
Elsa: *Yes, it would help a little bit, but I need a fence there.*
DT: *You need a fence to keep him away from you?*
Elsa: *Yah. Because I'm happy on that bit, you know, I'm living the dream and then you come and spoilt it.*
DT: *Spoilt it with my cowboy and his big old boots. You know he is shorter than your Gilgamesh statue, don't you?*
Elsa: *Yeah, but I'm lying down chilling out in the sun and vulnerable and happy, and I'm heavy with the gold, I'm really rich.*
DT: *But it feels vulnerable to be lying in the sun knowing there is a cowboy nearby. Why is it trampling is the first instinctive thing to come up?*

> Elsa: *Because it looks like he is running, and where is he going to go if I'm in front of him, he is going to go on top of me.*
> DT: *Then what happens?*
> Elsa: *I can drown in the sand or get invisible.*
> DT: *That is an interesting statement. What does invisible mean in this case?*
> Elsa: *Not being in the sand pit anymore, you've become the powerful one'.*

In the unconscious here then is the idea that the other is powerless against a patriarchal symbol. For Elsa, it is a reaction against that fear of being powerless which has driven her to achieve so much in her own life, which she acknowledged separately. For Elsa, this included her building her own company, and doing things her way.

This feeling of powerlessness though contrasts greatly with a symbol of Gilgamesh. One of the important things about the story or the myth of Gilgamesh is that he was a hero of ancient Mesopotamian mythology and was very much revered through the Epic of Gilgamesh, which was an epic poem written during the second millennium BC (Sandars, 1973). Whilst there are all sorts of ideas as to who Gilgamesh may have been, or who he represented, Gilgamesh is very much presented as a demigod with superhuman strength, who embarks on many journeys, famously defeating many different obstacles.

The use of symbolism here for Elsa is that Gilgamesh lies almost buried in the sand, the power of such a heroic archetypal symbol diminished or repressed through the mere appearance of a Lego man in a cowboy hat. The symbolic meaning of this should not be underestimated. Elsa was a participant with obvious will and power. She took her work incredibly seriously and developed a position whereby she could influence and assist children around her in many varying ways. To then encounter myself, even through my research such as it was, invoked within her a fear of the patriarch which led to her having to repress her will and power.

The connection between her world and that of Dianna's is also important to recognise. These internalised symbols of power and strength of the instinctual nature and of the hero are singularly contained or fearful of the power and the weight that stands before them. I could surmise that the fear of my presence as a man, as a patriarch, is what led to both of these women rejecting and ignoring their intersectional weight and power.

This theme of self-disempowerment was highlighted further in astonishing fashion via the lens of the sand tray exercise that was conducted in my own interview. To repeat, as part of my research, I undertook my own heuristic and creative exploration of the experiences of being the other. This meant that the questions and exercises asked of my participants were also repeated in my own interview by a colleague. In this instance, for myself I chose a white man, for my interviewer I selected a tall black woman, and for the relationship, I selected a pterodactyl (a third symbol selected to explore the space in between the pair of us, and a symbol selected intuitively which will be explored more in Chapter 5). When asked to select items by the interviewer and to explain why I had selected a pterodactyl I offered the following explanation:

> 'Pterodactyl is about to take off and that's the only thing I can say – although he is partly buried in the sand ... when I first put him in there, he was a lot deeper in the sand. Um ... Not sure, just ... mmmm ... actually he looks slightly fearful. Intimidated slightly. I don't know. Yeah. We'll go with that – intimidated'.

The burying of the pterodactyl in the sand is important as it speaks of an aspect of our relationship which has been made unconscious or suppressed and is seemingly about to emerge. Building on this point, we then went on to discuss the symbol of the white man:

> 'Yeah, a bit of fear or holding back in some way. I think there is some fear. There is some holding back in that figure. I actually want to say as well. This, his right hand looks like it wants to lash out at someone, like he is preparing to slap something'.

Here we see the internalised coloniser rage as directed at the black African woman, who seems to hold all of the power in the tray. The rage of myself as an internalised white man here speaks of both the anger that I had at an aspect of myself based upon my being encouraged to fit in with the majority, and also the fear and anger of the objectifier towards that which has been objectified. There is a fear here of the power that she holds in her deportment, with the woman looking elegant and proud whilst the white man seems clumsy and angry. In an attempt to get me to access that power temporarily, I was then invited to speak as a black woman (Figure 3.5):

> *DT:* How interesting. I am a tall elegant powerful black woman. I do my job every day. I am very in touch with the land around me. I am very loyal to my family and to my culture, to my tribe. Why me? I want to say. Hmmm.
>
> *I:* Tell me about your power.
>
> *DT:* It's simple really. I am it. I am that power. I don't have to try too

> hard. What I do and how connected I am to the world around me is my power. I get power from the water I drink, and I give back power in praise and thanks.

The importance of the three symbols together is that they show just how inauthentic I had become as the other in order to fit in with a majority through the suppression of my black identity and 'making myself white' in the

Figure 3.5 Dwight's Sand Tray.

process. This idea held echoes of one posited by Davids (2012), who although he doesn't utilise creative means to understand this process acknowledges its presence. It is also important here to notice the projection of the contra-sexual other onto my interviewer in this exercise. In this context, the images here of the dinosaur and the projection of power onto the black woman tie in with the earlier realisation of powerless against the subject presented by both Elsa and Dianna.

Although I will discuss this more in Chapter 5, it is important to recognise that much of this splitting when it occurs is actually quite traumatic, be they through incidents of racism, homophobia, sexism, and so on. As presented here in these sand trays, the trauma from these can run quite deep into the psyche, leaving an individual or a group questioning their own sense of who they are and their reality (Eom, 2014; Homeyer & Sweeney, 2011; Mayes et al., 2004). This is important, especially when we consider how it is often those individuals or groups who have been through trauma who then go ahead and reconstitute the abuses of others because of their own unresolved issues around the hatred meted out upon them in the name of patriarchal superiority, class superiority, or racial supremacy.

Where this differs for Elsa for example, is that her use of power was not then passed out and misused with somebody else. In her case, her wisdom and strength led to her using her power to set up her own organisation where she supported the child as the other. For Dianna though, this worked in a slightly different fashion. Dianna, whilst although willing to engage with myself, was very difficult to track down after our meetings and would often only reply at the very last minute before taking my research to the next stage. There was with Dianna a sense that she was not only afraid of myself, but that the material brought up within her was quite potent and very powerful. My suspicion in both instances was that something quite young had been triggered within them through our work in the sand tray. What we are talking about here, when we look at issues of supremacy, is that not only are these internalisations quite early on in life, as we explored in Chapter 2, but when they are activated within a therapeutic context then it is a very young part of oneself which can often react or act out accordingly.

My initial thoughts in trying to explore this wounded part of the psyche were actually to call it 'A wounded child'. My idea was based around the fact that these wounds can often occur at a very early stage of one's development. This though feels as if it minimises the full adultified impact of said experience. Whereas an inner child can be seen as not just innocent but also incredibly intelligent, the internalised abuser in comparison is limited through the lack of resolution of the trauma that they have endured (Zehnder & Calvert, 2004). As stated in Chapter 2, it is not uncommon for those who have endured the genderised trauma of patriarchy to then go ahead and abuse other minority groups. This may be presented under the guise of self-protection or protection of a whole grouping but is more often than not actually a facet of their own unresolved traumatic experience internalised and acting itself out from within one's own unconscious.

As also stated in that chapter, it is not uncommon for cultures who have been through their own traumatic experiences to then minimise the experiences of other cultures adjacent or close to them or within their own borders, in an attempt to control, denigrate, or force them to integrate into their own society. This is how supremacy and trauma beget supremacy through trauma. The individual though has to be very careful about their own internalised abuser. The internalised patriarch, the internalised racial supremacist, or the internalised capitalist will engage in the same behaviours presented in Chapter 2 in Figure 2.1 as any of the others higher up the chain. In understanding this internalised abuser that bit more, this internalisation has rejected the realities of others relying instead upon its own self-contained realities and ideas about itself. This is where this also leads to self-creative ideas and therefore conspiracy theories. Conspiracy theories in these instances are fantasies about the world around us and in particular about the others around us, whereby we believe stories that we have created. We choose not to check out said stories with the other because to discuss those with the other may lead to these stories being proven to be wrong which therefore leads to the bursting of the fantasy bubble created around the internalised abuser's wound.

A perfect and obvious example from a psychotherapeutic perspective came through a client of mine whose parents had split when he was quite young and who had been left with his father instead of his mother. The most obvious wound, that sense of rejection by his mother then appeared in every single relationship that he had and whereas at times he would often find himself drawn to women who did leave, even if often their reasons for doing so were fairly normal. Yet when they stayed, he would often spend hours, if not days, trying to find ways to prove that these people would ultimately desert him, and often within this self-created ideology of rightness would provoke said the experience so that the other, in these cases his partners, would continue to do exactly that.

The other factor within this particular case is the confirmation bias that sat within his wounded psyche. Confirmation bias here is not just the term used within psychology whereby researchers who hold a particular perspective on a research topic then seek out, be it consciously or unconsciously, material which confirms their ideas thereby not really engaging in research but engaging in a self-directed exploration of ideas which emphasises that they were right all along (Peters, 2020). Confirmation bias for the client followed a similar pattern, whereby he would often seek out material, ideas, and so on as a means of confirming that his partners were about to leave, or they were cheating on him.

When we consider though the moral aspect of the internalised abuser, morality in these instances is driven by the internalisation of said abuser. Because of a lack of morality within the original abuser, a consequence of the trauma upon the person or group on the receiving end is that their own moral compass has become distorted. So for my client, his inability to recognise the fact that when he left the relationship, he did so via text message, the ghosting of the other being his way of just leaving without any sort of comeback or any sort of emotional challenge. Several weeks late, he received a letter from his former partner whereby she expressed her distress, her pain, and her anger at what he had done, especially given that she had brought him into her life, and he had met not just her, her family but also her children. The client felt especially bad about this and in our exploration, whilst I was not there to judge him on it, my sense was it was a positive thing that he felt bad about what he had done to another person. He had not been able or brave enough to say what was going on for him, he had absolved himself from his moral responsibility for their relationship. In not being emotionally deep enough, he had denied himself, and her children, the chance to actually have a proper farewell and to be able to go their separate ways with their heads held high. For most of us, morality is about attempting to do the right thing. Yet, when things are very difficult, for somebody who internalised the abuser what actually exists is a propensity towards selfishness and doing what is easiest, being it to remove oneself from a scenario that they are no longer in control of, or to create the ways and means to deny the existence of the other.

Summary

This chapter has looked to explore the psychology of supremacy. As we have explored in previous chapters and also in the early part of this one, patriarchy, capitalism, and white supremacy, the three pillars of supremacy that I am talking about in this volume, all enact their influence upon the untouched psyche of a child from the moment they are born. in many ways, these are passed on even prebirth as well, through the parents and care givers for said children. It is therefore almost impossible for any child to ignore or resist the influences placed upon them within such situations.

This chapter also considered how these cultural adaptations actually have at their very roots critical narratives which underpin them. The structures of supremacy, as I have stated already, are reinforced through the cultural narratives of the day, narratives which would previously have been dictated by the various religions, but which are now more so dictated by laws and structures of the worlds that we live within.

Whilst the client examples presented here also allow one to explore and understand the supremacy complex, and whilst the Jungian narrative helps us to see just how hard the unconscious Self works in order to try and re-establish a true sense of being, what should also be noted is that this process is often quite painful as one stares into the abyss of one's own cultural gender, racial, ableist, homophobic, stereotypes and predilections that one has imbibed.

The use of creativity has also proven to be an important factor in exploring some of this material, and sand tray, whilst a seemingly simplistic way of working with the unconscious, is an unobtrusive form of exploration that not only bypasses the conscious logical structures of ego but allows one to understand these metaphorical internalisations in a non-traumatic fashion. For example, when I spoke to Elsa about the nature of Gilgamesh, she was surprised to see that she had so much power within her, surprised and also pleased I should add. To be able to reveal to clients that this is a part of who they are, that they are more than just the social constructionist adaptations, offers a type of psychological reparation that our work as therapists may not have assumed was possible without this type of deeper consideration.

That is not to say that this is easy. In my own processes, and as I have tried to explore what I have internalised, the fact that I may have uncovered one aspect one week, does not mean that I have not reverted back to a psychological adaptation the next. This exploration continues as we move to a philosophical exploration of supremacy.

References

Aboud, F. E. (1988). *Children and Prejudice*. Basil Blackwell Limited.

Aboud, F. E. (1993). The developmental psychology of racial prejudice. *Transcultural Psychiatric Research Review*, *30*, 229–242. 10.1177/136346159303000303

Berer, M. (2019). No title. *Medical Law International*, *19*(4), 258–281. 10.1177/0968533220914070

Bobo, L. (2017). Racism in Trump's America: reflections on culture, sociology, ad the 2016 US presidential election. *British Journal of Sociology*, *68*(S1), S85–S104. 10.1111/1468-4446.12324

Bowlby, J. (1973). *Separation*. Pimlico.

Bowlby, J. (1988). *A Secure Base: Parent-Child Attachment and Healthy Human Development*. Basic Books. 10.1097/00005053-199001000-00017

Brighi, E., & Cerella, A. (2015). An alternative vision of politics and violence: introducing mimetic theory in international studies. *Journal of International Political Theory*, *11*(1), 3–25. 10.1177/1755088214555455

Cherry, M. A., Downing, Jr., E., & Smith, B. W. (2019). *Hair Love*. Sony Pictures Animation.

Cox, M., & Thielgaard, A. (1986). *Mutative Metaphors in Psychotherapy: The Aeolian Mode*. Tavistock.

Davids, M. F. (2012). Internal racism: a psychoanalytic approach to race and difference by. *British Journal of Psychoanalysis*, *28*(4), 539–542.

Diangelo, R. (2018). *White Fragility: Why It's So Hard for White People to Talk About Racism*. Beacon Press.

Eom, M. (2014). Water: a symbol of potential. *Journal of Symbols & Sandplay Therapy*, *5*(1), 30–35. 10.12964/jsst.130015

Fredrickson, B. L., & Harrison, K. (2005). Throwing like a girl: self-objectification predicts adolescent girls' motor performance. *Journal of Sport & Social Issues*, *29*(1), 79–101. 10.1177/0193723504269878

Goodman, A. (970). Owain Glyn Dwr before 1400. *Welsh History Review1*, 5, 67–70.

Gordon, K. H., & Dombeck, J. J. (2010). The associations between two facets of narcissism and eating disorder symptoms. *Eating Behaviors*, *11*(4), 288–292. 10.101 6/j.eatbeh.2010.08.004

Government, H. (2010). *Equality Act 2010, Chapter 15* (Issue 1). https://doi.org/ISBN 978-0-10-541510-7

Hamilton, N. (2014). *Awakening Through Dreams: The Journey Through the Inner Landscape*. Karnac Books Ltd.

Haug, F. (2008). Memory work. *Australian Feminist Studies*, *23*(58), 537–541. 10.1 080/08164640802433498

Hodges, R. (2021). Defiance within the decline? Revisiting new Welsh speakers' language journeys. *Journal of Multilingual and Multicultural Development*, *0*(0), 1–17. 10.1080/01434632.2021.1880416

Homeyer, L. E., & Sweeney, D. S. (2011). *Sandplay Therapy: A Practical Manual*. Routledge.

Jakimowicz, S., Perry, L., & Lewis, J. (2021). Bowen family systems theory: mapping a framework to support critical care nurses' well-being and care quality. *Nursing Philosophy*, *22*(2). 10.1111/nup.12320

Jones, M. E. (1998). An invidious attempt to accelerate the extinction of our language. *Welsh History Review*, *19*(1), 226–229.

Jung, C. G. (1997). *Jung on Active Imagination* (J. Chodorow (ed.)). Routledge.

Kalff, D. M. (1991). Introduction to sandplay therapy. *Journal of Sandplay Therapy*, *1*(1), 1–4.

Kinouani, G. (2021). *Living While Black: The Essential Guide to Overcoming Racial Trauma*. Ebury Press.

Kirschner, S. R. (2012). How not to other the other (and similarly impossible goals: scenes from a psychoanalytic clinic and an inclusive classroom. *Journal of Theoretical and Philosophical Psychology*, *32*(4), 214–229. 10.1037/a0030158

Leonardo, Z. (2004). The color of supremacy: beyond the discourse of "white privilege." *Educational Philosophy and Theory*, *36*(2), 137–152.

Lowe, F. (2008). Colonial object relations: going underground black-white relationships. *British Journal of Psychotherapy*, *24*(1), 20–33. 10.1111/j.1752-0118.2 007.00061.x

Mackinnon, I. (2017). Colonialism and the highland clearances. *Northern Scotland*, *8*(1), 22–48. 10.3366/nor.2017.0125

Mayes, C., Blackwell Mayes, P., & Williams, E. (2004). Messages in the sand: sandtray therapy techniques with graduate students in an educational leadership program. *International Journal of Leadership in Education*, *7*(3), 257–284. 10.1080/13 603120410001694540

Mitchell, J. (1986). *The Selected Melanie Klein*. Penguin Limited.

Moustakas, C. (1994). *Phenomenological Research Methods*. Sage Publications.

Orgler, H. (1973). *Alfred Adler, The Man and His Work: Triumph Over the Inferiority Complex*. Sidgwick and Jackson.

Peters, U. (2020). What Is the Function of Confirmation Bias? *Erkenntnis*, *0123456789*. 10.1007/s10670-020-00252-1

Ram, M. (2014). White but not quite: normalizing colonial conquests through spatial mimicry. *Antipode*, *46*(3), 736–753. 10.1111/anti.12071

Sandars, N. (1973). *The Epic of Gilgamesh* (Revised ed). Penguin Classics.

Schaverien, J. (2005). International journal of art therapy. *The Journal of Analytical Psychology International Journal of Art Therapy*, *50*(102), 39–52. 10.1080/174548305 00345959

Schubert, M. (n.d.). *The "German nation" and the "black Other": social Darwinism and the cultural mission in German colonial discourse.* 10.1080/0031322X.2011.624754

Turner, B. A. (2005). *The Handbook of Sandplay Therapy.* Tenemos Press.

Unknown (2014). *Margaret Thatcher's Criticism of Brixton Riot Response Revealed.* BBC Website. http://www.bbc.co.uk/news/uk-30600064

Valdés Miyares, J. R. (2017). On the trail of the highland clearances: the clearances metanarrative in Scottish historical fiction. *English Studies*, *98*(6), 585–597. 10.1080/ 0013838X.2017.1322384

Various (2016). *The Bible: New King James Version.* Thomas Nelson.

Way, L. (1956). *Alfred Adler: An Introduction to His Psychology.* Penguin Books Limited.

Weil, A. M., & Piaget, J. (1951). The development in children of the idea of the homeland and of relations to other countries. *International Social Sciences Journal*, *3*, 561–578.

Williams, M. T., Holmes, S., Zare, M., Haeny, A., & Faber, S. (2022). An Evidence-Based Approach for Treating Stress and Trauma due to Racism. *Cognitive and Behavioral Practice.* 10.1016/j.cbpra.2022.07.001

Wurmser, L. (2015). Primary shame, mortal wound and tragic circularity: some new reflections on shame and shame conflicts. *The International Journal of Psychoanalysis*, *96*, 1615–1634. 10.1111/1745-8315.12470

Zehnder, S. M., & Calvert, S. L. (2004). Between the hero and the shadow: developmental differences in adolescents' perceptions and understanding of mythic themes in film. *Journal of Communication Inquiry*, *28*(2), 122–137. 10.1177/019685 9903261797

Zeigler-Hill, V., Clark, C. B., & Pickard, J. D. (2008). Narcissistic subtypes and contingent self-esteem: do all narcissists base their self-esteem on the same domains? *Journal of Personality*, *76*(4), 753–774. 10.1111/j.1467-6494.2008.00503.x

Chapter 4

The Philosophy of Supremacy

In February of 2022, during a global pandemic which led to lockdowns in countries across the world, the news item entitled Partygate was reaching a crescendo (Mason, 2022). For the past few months prior to this, the British press had taken to task the Tory Government of the day for having numerous gatherings and parties, all of these held in contravention of COVID-19 rules and regulations they themselves had put in place in order to protect the British population they represented (Mason, 2022). These parties, which dated back to the earliest days of the pandemic in the United Kingdom and stretched all the way through the next 18 months, were seen as a symptom of a growing realisation within the British population that they had been misled. The British public began to recognise that whilst they themselves had been told to obey certain rules and structures, those who were in charge, those who I would say were their political superego, chose to do something to benefit themselves.

There was another more subtle element to these news stories, in that this global pandemic though was to affect a disproportionate number of people from minorities across the Global North. In the United Kingdom, the rates of death within black, African, and Asian communities were that bit higher than within white communities (Various, 2020). Those who were less financially buoyant or from a different or lower class structure often found themselves having to risk their lives in order to maintain any level of well being and survive on whatever meagre resources they could find, whilst those with a certain class or capitalist privilege were able to lockdown outside the major cities often in places newly purchased (Woskie & Wenham, 2021).

To date, the pandemic has therefore hit the lower classes far more severely than any other group. A perfect example is a story told to me by my client Clare, a white, working-class woman originally from the Midlands. When she moved to London she settled with a partner, and they got themselves a small rental in a high rise in central London. For them, the whole process of Lockdown was a nightmare in they resided with their two young children, within a two-bedroom flat on the fifth floor of a large block in a council run estate. Being kept indoors for hours at a time on a day-to-day basis meant that she found her mental health suffering. This, therefore, led to us doing a

DOI: 10.4324/9781003313229-4

good number of our sessions online over Zoom, when we were able to do so and it was safe for Clare to have her sessions.

This chapter will explore some of the politics behind supremacy and will also consider how our profession has, perhaps inadvertently, collapsed into the thrall of a capitalist network and is therefore as guilty of exclusion as any other profession in the global north. Then we will look at what I will term The Superiority Drive, looking at how this is constructed and maintained, before offering a consideration as to how we can philosophically understand our ideas of supremacy. Then finally this chapter will look at how creatively exploring the philosophical perspective on supremacy offers a perfect route beyond said structures to a place whereby we might exist on a more equal plane.

First of all, though, this chapter looks to explore The Politics of Supremacy.

The Politics of Supremacy

One of the important factors to recognise when it comes to explorations around supremacy is the idea of morality and where this sits within the hierarchy that is supremacy. As a reminder, in Figure 3.2, although there are different rings which all locate themselves around a central ideology, person, or institution. Acolytes are those people who will sit around that central psition and maintain their superiority. In order for this to happen though, one then has to give up one's own sense of morality. What this actually means is that one's own inner sense of right and wrong becomes divorced from the individual or the group. Responsibility for this sense of morality is then passed inwards, where rules, structures, and fixtures are put in place to maintain any sense of superiority and safety that centrality may provide.

For the Acolyte, their loyalty to the centre also involves a displacement of their own sense of goodness. Goodness is then passed into the middle from where it can be used against the other at the other end of the scale accordingly. This is where conflicts start to arise. Morality and goodness then become concepts which can be co-opted by an individual, a group, a family, or a political party and then used against a marginalised other. The philosopher Gramsci in a paper by Jones (2006) recognised that this divorce from one's own sense of authenticity, rightness, and goodness is something that is not just given up by the Acolyte but which is something that is also coerced from the centre itself. In the modern age and in particular in this age of misinformation and manipulation, this is what seems to be happening, where civil societies repeat a certain narrative about the other. In conjunction with this, the idea that the centre proffers safety, therefore, encourages the Acolyte into a position of supplication whereby their give up their own authenticity and centrality and become part of a co-opted centre.

Conversely, the other in its recognition that it needs to be seen as right in order for it to be accepted and for it to be safe, becomes performative (Butler,

1988; Ram, 2014). Or it is annihilated in some implicit or explicit fashion. Looking at this through the lens of climate change, one can see this when we speak about the ideas behind greenwashing. To explore morality further, greenwashing as cited in papers by Delmas and Burbano, and Markham et al (2011; 2014) involves major companies and corporations selling the idea that they are doing more for the environment than they are in reality. What they point out is that in an attempt to corner increasing sectors of the market share, these attempts to appear green, and to promote themselves as more eco-friendly than they actually are, have led to many companies either overstating their green credentials or telling outright untruths. In these instances, the organisation has therefore taken the moral central ground and manipulated the acolytes into buying into their morality, and therefore their ideas. Greenwashing therefore also involves the continued flow of profits to the said organisation, whereby they do not have to necessarily do anything more to help the environment. The fact that they are talking and projecting a good ideal is enough for many of the Acolytes to fall into line behind them.

This is where goodness also comes into play. There is a belief for the Acolyte that they are doing the right thing, that they are being good, that they are being righteous, and one can also feel the religious element to this in the background. What one also has to realise though, when one buys into the greenwashing that maintains a company's capitalist centrality, is that the Acolyte is as much at fault for the climate's deterioration in this particular instance as the company is for not doing what it needs to morally do in order to provide sustainable produce for its customers. In giving up its own responsibility to either work towards the betterment of the planet itself or to hold the company to account, the capitalised colonised mind in these instances is unwilling to see for sure the detriment it is having upon the world around it (Zimmerman, 2020).

In a separate book on the topic, which considered the underlying psychological reasons why clients struggle to work with the issue of climate change in therapy, there is a suggestion that many of our clients may well appear in therapy unwilling to observe or consider how climate change has impacted upon themselves as if to do so would be painful existentially as well as psychologically (Various, 2013). Whilst I agree with this, what I also recognise is that the co-opted morality of the Acolyte has in many ways divorced itself in these instances from its own moral responsibility for the environment. This is not to say that we all must fight for the planet and nothing else, as it is incredibly difficult to do so. What this is to say is that the constant pull to the centre is like the pull of a black hole; it is very difficult to remove oneself from it, at best we hope to live alongside it, recognising its pull but still remembering that we have an obligation, a duty to others around us, our families, our friends, and the environment.

The Superiority Drive

Arising out of psychoanalysis and initially posited by Sigmund Freud in his book the Ego and the Id, drive theory remains a core, if not contested, component of psychoanalytical theory (Sletvold, 2013). Initially, this theory was used to understand aggressive behaviours between human beings. Freud initially saw this as being something of an internal force which fought against a sense of psychological balance within ourselves (Jacobs, 2003). Whilst I am not in this brief exploration going to consider the sexual nature of the drive, what I will say is that this drive to superiority fits a similar consideration when we factor in the idea that this is something we are all imbued within. The drive to be better, to be superior, to be the best, sits within most of us at some stage in life, be it that we want to be the best sports person, musician, artist, or that we want to write the best academic paper and receive the most awards, that drive to be at the top of our game is a core part of our human existence.

For this drive though to exist, and for the subject to see itself as superior, there also has to be a splitting off and a recognition of that which is deemed inferior accordingly. The Superiority Drive is therefore nothing without the need to compare oneself against another. It is a drive that will seek out another and use them in a way which might be unbeknownst to the other but may well still occasionally have a huge impact on the other's existence. The Superiority Drive and stereotyping or objectification or othering, which is a term I tend to use most often, run together. To briefly state, othering is a concept whereby instead of recognising that a person is a composite picture of intersectional identities, what we do is make that person less worthy of respect and of a moral response to their cause, or their malaise, by reducing them down into one or two key components which we, in turn, relate to from a superior position (Kirschner, 2012; D. Turner, 2016).

To talk about how this works, I would like to present a dream by a client called Clive. Clive was a 55-year-old white, semi-retired man. Considering himself middle class, he had made his fortune working in the City of London and had retired early. His presenting issue initially had to do with the fact that his partner had found out he was having an affair and had left him. In coming to see me for a few sessions though, although we worked with the issue of the separation between him and his partner, the other thing that became incredibly important in our work together was the fact of the multi layers of difference between myself and Clive in the therapy room. This came to a head at one point when Clive told me about a dream he had had.

In the dream, Clive was at Speaker's Corner. Stood on a soap box, he was talking loudly to a crowd of people about how to best invest their money and make the best out of their living. The crowd though were not listening to him. As Clive observed the crowd, he saw that there was a group of women who were sat around on the grass talking amongst themselves, whilst a man with

an obvious disability wandered past listening to music through his head-
phones. I was also in the dream, but I was seated upon a bench with someone
who, in the dream was my cousin, and we were talking amongst ourselves.

When I asked Clive how he felt about his position and the position of everybody else in the dream, what he realised was that he was angry and upset
that no one was paying him attention. He found his upset though becoming
fierier as we discussed this. Later in the session, he acknowledged that
actually in the dream what he wanted to do was to take the soap box and
throw it across at one group or another to make them pay him attention. He
wanted us all to listen to him because, according to the dream, he knew best.

What this dream though says in the context of this book is it highlights the
hierarchical nature of supremacy. As an older, middle class, white heterosexual man, Clive had taken on the identity of the patriarch, yet from within
this role, this socially constructed experience of the dream showed him
something very different; that his power was not absolute and that there was
no other for him to dominate.

The second thing about the Superiority Drive is that it is also strangely
based upon a dualistic fear. What I mean by this is that in an encounter with
difference, the first emotion to inevitably rise to the surface is one of wariness
and fear. We, therefore, resort to a defensive kind of superiority, one which is
about adopting a position not just to dominate the other, but to manage our
own fear of another we have no real experience. So, whereas domination
involves the triple blades of supremacy, othering, and power, when we feel a
sense of fear towards the other, whilst power may be involved again, what we
also do is try to marginalise and reject said other.

An important example of this is the emergence of the European powers
and their encounters with different cultures as part of the colonial project.
The movement into the indigenous north of America, an encounter that led
to the annihilation of millions of First Nation Americans, was as much based
upon a need to dominate as it was on an existential type of fear (Dudley,
2017). This fear of another also sits behind the need to subjugate the other.
For example, the invisibility of the other therefore keeps the subject safe from
its own sense of fear, a fear of being annihilated and a fear of being destroyed.
Yet, when the other then returns, or finds its voice, or chooses to speak up,
for the subject this fear then leads to an acting out which I believe is a core
facet of the Superiority Drive.

To offer another angle, DiAngelo's (2018) work around the fragility of
whiteness is important. To explore the idea here, for DiAngelo white fragility
involves the fragility of the egoic sense of self that white people experience
when they encounter or have to work with issues around race and difference.
A very popular idea culturally, my own belief is that this perspective whilst
well-meaning does not quite work. What has always been missing is a
broadening of the narrative around encounters with the socially constructed

other, and therefore an understanding of just how any encounter with difference leads to a reactivity of the socially constructed ego of the subject. A subject which could be any one of us, as we are all of us simultaneously the other and the subject.

A first date with a potential new partner that we have only seen on an internet website will bring fear because they are different from us, and we do not know them. In the same way that any engagement with the other on a cultural level leads to a sense of fear that one will be swamped and one's culture will be decimated by the grounding of the cultural other within our country. Whilst if, as von Franz (1980) stated, the other is all around us and that we can project upon to the other, both individually and collectively aspects of our own discarded shadow, then fragility, white, gendered, homophobic, or otherwise, at its core is a defence against the shadow returning home.

As I have stated, there are a couple of ways for the subjects to manage this experience when meeting the other. In my own encounters when I have spoken up about difference and otherness, one of the most interesting comments that I get in return is often the fear that what I say comes from an angry place. I even recall speaking to a colleague about the Black Lives Matter movement, where said colleague stated that one of the things that he was most worried about was the sense that most white people were afraid that black people would come after them and kill them all.

The Superiority Drive is therefore as much driven by fear as it is by a need to be superior and on our training courses there are numerous instances where discussions about difference and otherness have led to a reactivity against any exploration by those in the opposing subjective team. Perfect examples emerge out of group discourses where when the minoritised group is encouraged to speak out, those who are unaware of their own unconscious superiority will then take offense, will act out, or will simply burst into tears. This is not so much to do with a sense of fragility, in my opinion, as with a need to create an opposition and therefore a need to regain any sense of superiority.

The Philosophy of Supremacy

The philosophy of the Subject's idea of the Other has been a core component of philosophy for hundreds of years. Yet, it is an idea that has in the past 150 years or so been challenged a lot by more contemporary philosophical ideas. This shift opens the door to making not only philosophy and our philosophical understanding of humanity more phenomenological. Whilst also recognising, I will argue here, that the dualistic ideas which have riddled philosophy have recreated and reinforced some of the hierarchies of meaning sat within it. This move away from a dualism which sat central to Descartian ways of viewing our existence allows room for some of the ideas of the brilliant philosopher Spinoza (1996). In his work Ethics, perhaps his most famous collection of papers, Spinoza laid out an argument against Descartes' ideas of dualism. His idea was that there is a natural flow to and from God and that our very human perceptions of this ultimate truth were not only imperfect, but they were faulty. For Spinoza, whilst we are in relationship with the other, be it each other or the world around us, there is a constant striving within us towards a more perfect and moral standard of truth that benefits us all. In my view, Spinoza's ideas edge us towards a more moralistic standpoint in how we relate to each other, and they counteract this destructive drive to dominate the other, to obtain Godhood through a sense of superiority.

One of the interesting things about Spinoza's ideas is that although they may appear hierarchical, what they also involved is the idea of transcendence (James, 2014). That is to say in this instance when we incorporate a more psychotherapeutic angle, the transcendence of previous ways and ideas of being. Transcendence though is a problematic word and, whilst I can agree with Spinoza's intention, I think perhaps a combination of this and a more Buberian way of understanding the subject and the other, especially the internalised aspects of such, helps here. For Buber (2010), whilst the subject and the other are tied together in an I-it relationship, he does not really recognise that there is a hierarchy involved. In fact, in many ways, Buber tends to ignore this. So, a combination of Buber's more esoteric writings, where the spiritual is accessed through the relationship between subject and object, when seen alongside Spinoza's visions, then takes us towards a more relational exploration of difference, together with a more relational understanding of just how one can understand and therefore possibly move beyond the internalised supremacist (Buber, 1952).

For other theorists and philosophers such as Levinas (Hand, 2009; 2006) a slightly more malevolent aspect of relationship is overtly incorporated. For Levinas, the relationship with the other, whilst spiritual in nature holds within itself levels of cruelty and hatred which Buber seemed loathe to acknowledge. What all three though recognise is that our experiences of self are very much influenced by the surroundings we are born into. They recognise that human experiences, whilst phenomenological, as well as being natural and generated in relation to each other, were also socially constructed via the intersecting layers of privilege and oppression as explored in the previous chapters.

What I would say is also a second problem with the ideas of philosophers such as Spinoza and Levinas, is that their ideas tend to hint at identity being again a singular construct. To move beyond this and to therefore complicate the layers of intersecting supremacy that influence us at all times, we then have to start to recognise that our intersecting identities are multiple, numerous, and uncountable. Of all the theorists to perhaps enter into this realm of understanding, Deleuze and Guittari are perhaps some of the few to engage with this material in such a way (Deleuze & Guattari, 2013).

One of their core ideas was that we are all machines, constructs working within a system of other machines in a kind of endless conglomerate of meaning and that we all play a part in the whole system to keep humanity moving forward at its own inexorable pace. Now, whilst their ideas of machines, and of machines within machines, is complex, it is also quite nuanced in its recognition of who we are as individuals and as groups and societies. One issue with Deleuze's ideas is that they very much explore identity in the form of machines as external to us looking at how all these machines jostle with each other for position and prominence within a larger, wider system. Holding echoes of system theory within the world of counselling and psychotherapy where a system could be anything from a family to a company to a class in a school, to a gang, these machines are activated by and active within an environment in which they influence and which influences upon them (Jakimowicz et al., 2021).

Seeing this through a metaphorical lens, like a forest full of trees, a forest is made up of millions of different plants and organisms all of which play their own separate role. Alongside this, each one of these organisms relies on the different plants and organisms all around it for it to fulfil the said role. The interaction is ongoing and apparent. In this instance though, there is no hierarchy. There is a conglomerate (I am choosing this word for a reason), that works together for the collective good. So, where a social construction, a hierarchy to be implemented, this would therefore suggest that certain trees, certain plants, and organisms have priority, have privilege, have supremacy over their cousins and their kin accordingly.

One other aspect that should be noted is that within each one of these organisms are numerous, hundreds, thousands, nay millions of other machines, other organisms, other aspects, other sub-personalities which all play their roles in creating, maintaining, and re-affirming the overall organism. Ultimately, we are incredibly complex beings. This more collective exploration of identity and our identities challenges social constructionist narratives of a singular subject and object, supremacy inferiority, and split. It is a constant factor as we internally wrestle back control of who we are as individuals, as clients, and as psychotherapists. Understanding how the triadic challenges of the patriarchal, white supremacist, capitalist ideologies have informed our super egoic senses of self and therefore moulded us is important as we ascertain just why we are either way more or way less than we are meant to be or than our potential. This means that individuation, a topic discussed in more detail in Chapter Five, is a movement outside of the grip of this triple-headed hydra of self-maintained oppression to a more expansive, potentially more infinite means of being.

Basically, what I am tracking here is the idea that the regular phenomenological route of subject and other, the Hegelian idea of a binary sense of self, is incomplete and in fact totally inadequate when it comes to trying to understand identity through an intersectional lens. The use of other theoretical and philosophical perspectives, therefore, allows us to broaden and in fact map out where aspects of our intersectional identities, plural, are influenced by the social constructions which are placed upon us from birth. Not all of these will be influenced, but often the parts which are the most troubled, and which enter into therapy trailing behind our clients as they look to understand their individual senses of self, accordingly, are the ones which hold our wounds. So, within this existential lens, human beings are very much machines, and these machines are of course intersectional. This bridge between a philosophy designed by black feminists out of a third wave of feminism and certain Western philosophers is therefore an obvious one for myself to make.

Another angle in this philosophical exploration emerges when we add the issue of power into the phenomenological mixture. Proctor (2010) in her work raises the spectre of three types of power. Linking her ideas around power to my exploration of supremacy, it seems obvious to suggest that one of her most interesting, that being power over the other, is most relevant to my ideas. Here I want to include though the ideas of Arendt (2018), whose immense works explored the role of the mundane and the supposed divorce from personal power to the institutional or systemic structures of power which then abuse and annihilate the other. Through a combination of these two ideas, and when coupled with those already presented in this and previous chapters, we already begin to see how power, when not owned, and when not disabused of the reactive force of supremacy, then becomes destructive. For Arendt, the simplicity of this psychological divorce, the ease which with a Subject rejects its own morality, then leads potentially to destruction. Where this might appear in the therapeutic world is in the continued ignorance of the impacts of supremacy's often politically instructed triumvirate upon those minoritised groups, or in the therapy room by the use of behaviours and language which harm, offend or reject the other.

These ideas also tie themselves to the perspectives of other philosopher's, such as Rousseau (1984) who saw the self, or the individual which is what I believe he meant, as indivisible from the whole. He also saw that the whole held within its structures of the political. The self here then becomes part of the larger machine as already discussed, both playing a part within said machine as well as being a core component of any actions it takes against the other. In a strange way, the self here does not dominate the machine, except in its refusal to accept the moral responsibility placed within all self's. This abdication of morality, together with the rejection of access to its own power, means that all decision making, all wisdom, and guidance, is passed out of the hands of so many to be held centrally by the hands of the few.

An example on an individual level comes out of a client I once had who regularly wanted me to affirm her beauty. Week after week she would come in and ask me if I thought she was attractive, beautiful, and sensual. If I did not answer, then the questions became more subtle. They changed in their language, but never in their objective. My countertransference was always one of annoyance, especially as the questions were often repeated several times. Yet, I held my boundaries as much as I could, and used my supervision so I didn't react, or act into the therapy in any way. In the end, her frustration with me bubbled to the surface. It was then I was able to help the client use that ire, that fire, and help her to re-empower herself. Eventually, this ignited a type of self-love or esteem, she had been unaware of before, and she was able to take this away with herself. Her projected power had returned home to its host.

Now, the reason for presenting that brief client example is to highlight three things. First, I am a therapist, and being able to hold and work with the divorce between the client and their power to is an important aspect of all our works. It is there all the time. The second is to continue to raise awareness of the responsibility of therapists to be aware of their own relationships to power. Should this not have been assessed, explored, or at least contained, then there is good reason to assume that the therapist will be more prone to acting out the power dynamics in the therapy room in an unhealthy fashion. The third, and most important one for this book, is to ask the reader to see this on a larger scale. If, Rousseau's self is multiplied by millions, and those millions have rejected their own power, then that overburdening or co-opting of power by forces outside of them becomes inevitable. This misuse of power on a collective scale is all our responsibilities.

The corruption of this collective responsibility has been seen in everything from the Brexit vote in the United Kingdom, to the election of Far-Right Nationalist or Populist governments in countries across the Global North. Coupled with the divide and fear tactics utilised by most governments, where there is another created to hate, as well as within families in a different fashion, where one member of the family is scapegoated, this now centralised power remains in-situ until it is taken back by the populace.

Therapeutically, when we combine the varying forms of intersectional philosophical discourses, we begin to see that when power is taken away by another group that the ability to self-define, to be oneself, or even to individuate, is stunted. There will be aspects of one's intersectional identity which will remain in distress.

The continued divestment of power, often after the active theft or the use of such against the other, then holds within it the ongoing pain of oppression within systemic regimes and structures. Conversely, the origins of Political Correctness, the origins of the Woke movement, are attempts to take back control, to regain power, within the political arms of these intersectional structures. There are movements here to wrest power back into the collective and individual palms of the other, away from the collective superego as discussed in chapter three, Figure 3.1.

This is why clients occasionally come to therapy. They are not always wholly ill. An aspect of their intersectional identity is no longer functioning as the constraints of the socially constructed system desire it to. Our job is to therefore understand the reasons why that aspect is no longer functioning. Our job is to also understand the socially constructed systems in place which provided protection against any change; this is where the systems of oppression appear. A working class client bound within a patriarchal capitalist structure who struggles to find their own voice amongst their upper class colleagues; a woman who has been told to hate immigrants but wants to support those emergent out of the war in Ukraine; the man who wants to support Trans rights but is fearful of being shamed by his friends and colleagues; the child who refuses to eat meat at school yet is constantly being told they are weird if they do so by the teachers and their peers. These are all examples of the moral drive attempting to wrest power away from the centralised system of projected and real oppression. These are all real-world, real-life examples.

Therefore, I strongly believe one of the issues with philosophy in its modern format is that it often tends to other us all in our pursuit of control of who we are within our wider environments. The philosophers who have struggled to really engage with the problem of existence, and have done so from a more objective standpoint, have often lost the rest of us in their overly academic hierarchical and privileged language and way of seeing the environment. These are not the ones who have come down from the mount and translated their commandments for the populous. They are the ones who have stayed up on the mount and expected the rare few to brave and weather the wintery storms as they ascend to their pinnacle.

What I have done with that previous metaphor in some ways is not just to use philosophy as a means of understanding how supremacy sits within a philosophical framework, but also as a by-product of this to show how philosophy itself has bought into the supremacy of the cultural intellectual. To bring my ideas further down from the mount, the sense that Jean Paul Sartre brought to his works and in particular some of his more obscure works, such as Black Orpheus involved his allowing himself the range and the opportunity to explore the socially constructed racialised oppression of another through his own philosophical lens (Sartre & MacCombie, 1964). An interesting book, very different from many Sartre wrote (and also interestingly difficult to obtain) the ideas held within this tome will resonate widely with those persons of colour as Sartre clearly saw and explored the pain and oppression of blackness within a French colonial context.

This section, therefore, presents some philosophical ideas about the importance not just of understanding our intersectional identities, but also of understanding that when we bring in social constructions around the identities that we adopt, and when these adaptations begin to falter, or we desire to individuate, that these faulty adaptations will inevitably hinder the machine's ability to work to its potential. Like cancers that sit hidden, they gnaw away at aspects of who we are until they ultimately destroy us.

From Supremacy to Morality

The Supremacy Defence

Supremacy as a construct, as we have seen, is very much driven by the super egoic need to maintain control over the ego, its defences, and the social constructionist aspects of its identity. The superego, therefore, believes it is very much in control, it holds power and sways over its own domain but it also needs the other, an externalised other who, as Jung and von Franz would have said, play the part of the shadow for the ego (Johnson, 1993; Jung, 1990; von Franz, 1980). This binary conjuntio between the superego and ego can occur in many forms in a therapeutic space. The superiority defence is presented below in the following Figure 4.1.

To explore Figure 4.1, it is worth recognising the following defences which define the superiority defence. *All Knowing Ignorance* is the first of these. The idea that one can know everything about everything is an aspect of the superiority defence and defines it by failing to recognise that there are a myriad of ways and ideas and things that one does not, will not, and could not, ever know in our lifetime. This denial of possibilities is what sits behind such things as conspiracy theories, right wing rhetoric and perspectives on the world around us which have become absolute and defined. The interesting thing about this type of defence is that there is a level of ignorance built within it. Back in Chapter 2, when we explored the idea of history washing,

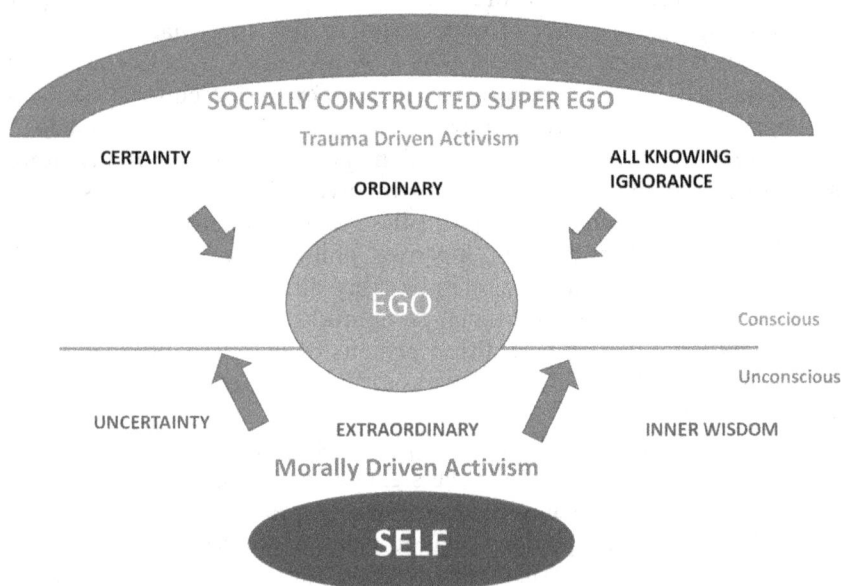

Figure 4.1 The Supremacy Defence.

what that also entails is an idea that actually for supremacy to exist, there are a finite number of ideas and things that one can and must know. The idea that science is always evolving, is always changing runs against the idea of supremacy, against the comfortable mirage that we are all all-knowing creatures.

The second defence in this triad is one of *Certainty*. An avoidance of the anxiety of the uncertain, of the unknown and unknowing, sits within this defence. The ego knows its place in the world, it knows the identity it should have and the identity of those around it. It knows what it is to be a man, what it is to be a woman, what it is to be LGBTQ, black, disabled. It denies that there is any other reality other than the one centred around itself. It therefore vilifies, puts down, denigrates anything which may threaten this delicate balance between superego and ego.

The third defence though, is probably the simplest one to explore, but also the most powerful. There is an ordinariness to this sort of person, group, organisation, culture, system as Hannah Arendt explored in her work around Eichmann. It was the ordinariness of this man; this was a man who had his own life, and family, had a career and who did quite a mundane and plain job, but in doing a job based within a system of certainty, of ignorance, a system which defined the Nazi project, he took up a role as ordinary and as simple as any of those in the offices around him.

To offer a more contemporary example, when we see the struggles of migrants in their attempts to cross the channel, what we often hear from perfectly ordinary people is a rhetoric of hate and denigration that they should even attempt to do such a thing, that they are coming to invade these shores. These perfectly ordinary people will be the same ones in private members' clubs in the United Kingdom, or working within a capitalist and patriarchal system, to make a living and to survive and make their way through life.

This following statement is what is most important about them: Evil as presented in films and media in anything from James Bond to Star Wars is not built upon the idea of something alternative, outlandish, and out there. Evil, by its very nature, is perfectly ordinary and resides within the super egoic, ego connection. It sits within the wilful ignorance of all of us, myself included, who deny the fact that we have a moral responsibility for the other. It sits within the unconscious anxiety within all of us, myself included, where we struggle with not knowing, where we crave certainty, the certainty of knowing where our next meal is coming from, out next relationship, the next hit. We want to know, we want to be held, and we want to feel safe. When we crave those things, be they individually or as part of a collective whereby we divest ourselves of responsibility for such and give it to our politicians, governments, job, whatever that might be, we give up on the inner drive to be more and are easily co-opted, corrupted and made to be part of said system of supremacy.

To move this though to a space opposite, one has to recognise that there are stages we all need to go through. The first one is simple, *Inner Wisdom*. Often when we hear stories about prejudice, sexism, homophobia, what is often pitched is that these people are ignorant and therefore all they need to do is to learn and they will change. Whilst this idea makes perfect sense on one level, and is sort of correct, what it fails to recognise though is that this wisdom is not just external. The whole reason for writing this particular book was to help the reader to recognise that any exploration, in fact, any excavation, in order to understand supremacy, would involve an inner knowledge needing to be discovered, explored, recognised, and owned. That also will involve spotting where our ignorance has informed our inactions and dealing with said shame and pain before coming to some sort of resolution with these facts.

The second part of this movement from the superego-ego dyad to one whereby the ego and the self-reconnect will actually involve the ability to sit with *Uncertainty*. It feels quite light to suggest as such as if this is just something one has to do, and it is a very easy thing. It is not. To be with the discomfort and the anxiety built within uncertainty is part of the existential route toward self-knowledge. When we sit with the fact that we do not know, the fact that we are uncertain of our place in the world, of what our work will do for now or for the future when we are moving forward to something which is way beyond ourselves.

What I mean by this statement though, is whenever one hears for example right or left winger state that they are on the right side of history, or they have got God on their side, what they are sort of saying is that they are certain that they are doing the right thing and that this certainty is what will drive them in the end towards victory. For any activist, for anyone who is doing this sort of work in rooting out and understanding their internalised social constructions of identity within a supremacist system, one of the biggest aspects of this said journey is to be able to sit with uncertainty, to reside in the existential anxiety provoking possibility that all this, that this fighting of the good fight, might have been for nought.

It is the last part though, of this triumvirate which is perhaps one of the more interesting ones to explore, it is the *Extraordinariness* of the journey that one must undertake. This involves recognising that any pathway towards self-knowledge, towards uncertainty, takes us outside of the ordinary structures defined and given to us in our early life and places us in a space of extraordinary phenomenological definitions of what it is to be a human being. When one sits outside of the persona's citadel of knowing, where one might go is undefined, unexpressed, and an undiscovered country. That, therefore, opens up a myriad of possibilities. Our inner wisdom then directs us towards something we have not recognised within ourselves before. It takes us out to help those who we may not have reached out to, or expressed an opinion towards, or even met on our journey where we safely ensconced inside the citadel. As we wander through the landscape of potentialities, the uncertainty that comes with not really knowing where we are going to end up next, who will look after us, and how we will be fed, gives us a deeper layer of self-understanding that we can use when we work with the other. The extra-ordinariness of the path that is laid before us gives us the chance to do things, be things, and create things that many of us would never have foreseen or foretold when we were growing up within our comfortable, ordinary, socially constructed environments.

The Symbolism of Supremacy

For this philosophical exploration of unconsciously internalised supremacy, it is also essential to create a means of working that both allowed a level of depth to understand and was also safe for participants. The reasons for this are, as previously stated, the socially constructed identities that we are talking about here were influenced by the triumvirate of capitalism, patriarchy, and white supremacy and actually sit quite deeply in the psyches of all of us. Therefore, to try and challenge them or to bring them to the surface, can often be quite traumatic for our clients, ourselves as therapists, and anyone else interested in this kind of shadow work.

Social constructions of identity bind the subject and the other together. Given this co-construction of identity and therefore worth, of course when one challenge or explores that aspect of identity, then its brother, its sister, its co-companion in this co-construction of identity and worth will of course be challenged accordingly. The defence is then raised within the subject. So, when there is a discussion around race by the racialised other, this will of course bring up lots of unconscious material for the racialised subject. Another example, when issues around patriarchy, sexism, and misogyny then come up in semi-safe spaces for women, then, of course, men, given the co-construction of their identity within a patriarchal system, will feel threatened accordingly. The interesting aspect within this is that the threat, that the reaction is often very unconscious and can often take the subject by total surprise. This is one of my key reasons for using sand play work.

Supremacy and Creativity: The Sand Tray Exercise

As previously stated, the sand tray is an established method for accessing unconscious material (Bradway, 2006). It was used in this study because, again, working with symbols allowed for the unconscious presentation of internal or repressed unconscious material around differences (Cox & Thielgaard, 1986). The exercise, which was designed by me, involved the participant selecting three objects from a thousand predetermined toys to represent themselves, myself, and our relationship. Building upon the ideas presented in Chapter Three, the design for the exercise took its direction from the Buberian idea that there as well as an I and thou/it position there is a third one, that was the in-between space, from where often springs creativity or spirituality (Buber, 2002). These toys would then be placed in a tray of sand. The exercise was chosen to move beyond the limitations of the verbal and connect with the pre-verbal, and perinatal, consciousness, crossing cultural, gender, sexual, and other boundaries and offering a more universal experience of an unconscious phenomena than say using just words might (Labovitz Boik & Anna Goodwin, 2000).

Another crucial consideration when working with symbols and sand tray in this context is its ability to hold the duality of 'psychic opposition' (B. A. Turner, 2005, p. 38). In this context, this brings us back to a consideration of the limitations of the dualistic perspectives of difference that are often presented from more political, developmental, or social perspectives, for example, and roots this particular work more within the relational vision of the transpersonal.

After selecting objects, participants were then invited to talk about their images in the sand tray, with the following questions acting as prompts (presented as Table 4.1).

It was also important for this research that my own experience as a researcher be logged, together with a close consideration of the impact my relationship with my participants and others may have had on me. This view arose from the sense that often, and especially within psychotherapy, the fact that the researcher is not present in the research in some way, could have been seen as a type of flaw to the results of the research itself (Romanyshyn, 2010). How do I see my participants? What are my projections onto them? How does my experience of them inform who I am now? If this is a relational exploration of supremacy, then given that as the researcher this same phenomenon was in the room right there and then, there would be a wealth of important additional research material which could be used in this study. In asking my participants to choose a symbol they felt represented myself, for the purpose of this exercise, I would therefore become an 'It' for my them (Buber, 2010), a blank screen for them to project whatever they needed to

Table 4.1 Co-Created Sand tray

Questions to the Client:
- Why have you selected these items? What do they mean to you?
- Why do you feel you have positioned these objects in this way?
- What do you feel these objects have to say about each other? How do they relate?
- What qualities do each of the objects have?
- Is there anything else you would like to say about your sand tray?

I then invited the participant to ask me, the researcher, the same set of questions before finally asking them the following.
- Are there any other questions you would like to ask?
- How do you view my sand tray?

onto me in that instance, much like the role a therapist would actively perform in more traditional psychodynamic psychotherapy (Winnicott, 1969). I therefore also chose three symbols allowing me to see just which aspects of myself I had projected onto my participants.

The first of my examples here, is Brodie. Brodie engaged with my research because he was interested in the experiences that he had had growing up young gay man in a suburb of Sao Paolo in Brazil. His family was quite wealthy, and they, therefore, sent him to a fairly good church school in the area where he was regularly bullied and picked on, his peers seeing him as overly feminine. Because this was a church school, he often used to have to attend bible studies as well, and even within this sort of more Catholic environment, Brodie found himself marginalised and picked on by his peers and by the priests within this church group, many of whom did not take to him.

By the time that Brodie reached middle school, for some unexplained reason, he realised he was the only boy in a class full of girls. His sense of feeling like an outsider was something that he walked with consistently throughout his life and was something that was passed on to him, not just through religion and culture, or by being an outsider in his middle school but also because he was influenced by a religious narrative which stated that his being gay was wrong, was bad and was immoral.

Another part of Brodie's story involved his deciding to travel for a week away to an island in Europe. Whilst he was there though, he quickly realised that the week he had chosen was actually Bear Week, and he was already again an outsider. He spent much of that week on his own listening to music on his iPod and sitting by the pool.

For the sand play exercise, Brodie chose a bear for me, a shaman for himself, and a hippo for our relationship. He says of the symbols (presented as Figure 4.2):

Brodie:	the first thing that came to me is when you said you know, choose an object for you, me, and the relationship, the first thing I thought is I really hope there's a bear for you, because I have the sort of bear, but the side of the bear that is sweet rather than the one that
DT:	that will scratch your throat out?
Brodie:	yeah. A sort of motherly figure in a sense, a bear, because that's how I perceive you, very gentle, caring and yeah, um, I just couldn't think of anything else, it just came straight away. Bang! There's a bear, you know. And, you know, very likeable animals, you know, bears you can think also of the polar bear, one of the most sorts of the, and of course there's the other side to a bear, but I don't know you enough to know what the other side is.

DT:	that's ok, don't worry.
Brodie:	in terms of me that was easy, the other two I really struggled with. The second one I finally found something, and that's because I see myself as a shaman, and I thought that's it, it was the one that picked my …
DT:	your attention, grabbed you
Brodie:	yeah, grabbed me. So, I thought that's a shaman, and then I just for the relationship, I don't know why I picked it, a hippo. I don't know why, I just suddenly thought 'that's cute, I'm gonna go for that'. I don't know what it is, but I just went for it. I don't know you that well, but there is something sweet in hippos, and they're very, I think now that I think about it, if you think phenomenologically about a hippo. Hippos are very ancient animals, they live in waters, but they live in the land as well, it's very, they're big but they are soft at the same time, they're not attacking. There's something sweet and soft in them, at the same time I have never seen any of them, so I think there is something of the really unknown, as I know you but really, I don't. it's a fascinating animal, and
DT:	makes a fair amount of sense
Brodie:	I don't know that's what I picked.
DT:	that's perfect. What else did you want to say?
Brodie:	I was going to say I put them close together, it didn't feel they belonged in the centre, I like them there in the corner, me and you and then this thing coming up out of us, and we're sort of guiding it.

Studying Brodie's Sand Tray

It is important to recognise Brodie's use of a bear, and his unconsciously having forgotten that it related back to Bear Week, are part of his story. To explore Bear Week slightly further, as Brodie states, this is a week whereby at a certain resort in Europe a number of gay men would congregate in order to socialise and enjoy the experiences relevant to their culture (Various, 2014). For Brodie though, being a slight man, he automatically felt that he did not fit in. As he states also in this tray of sand, for him bears and hippos are family-orientated animals; they are territorial. Whereas, the Shaman, the symbol he chose for himself, was a solitary soul, often sat outside of a tribe or a group. Exploring this further, anything of a more communal nature, anything which might have been deemed as being of the centre, has been projected onto myself in the form of the bear and hippo, whereas that more isolationist aspect and yet also incredibly wise part, sits within himself as an outsider.

Figure 4.2 Brodie's Sand tray.

There are echoes of the power afforded to the subject in the projections of the bear and the hippo onto me. There are also echoes of the true worth and power of the Shaman which resonate with Elsa's tray in Chapter 3, whereby her symbol of Gilgamesh of a symbol or character embedded in power and mythology is hugely important. The deeper worth, the deeper strength, the near spiritual archetypal sense of power which sits within Brodie's sand play work.

It is also important to note the positioning of the symbols in Brodie's tray. Brodie states in his narrative that he chose to place all his symbols in the corner of the tray for a reason. The placing of these symbols and in particular that of the hippos, suggests a fear of my side of the tray and helps us to recognise the power imbalance even in doing a piece of research like this.

Therapists recognising their power and especially the power afforded to them within socially constructed environments is massively important. Another way of looking at this within this instance is as a heterosexual man working with gay man, this may have unconsciously brought up that sense of socially constructed inferiority. The power imbalance is there, even though we have not overly talked about our sexual orientations.

For the next stage, we then explored my side of the tray:

DT:	alright, well I didn't know why I've gone for this. The car jumped out for myself, maybe that's me being on a journey and a bit old fashioned, this car. It's from the 20s and 30s sort of thing, probably not used to driving through sand. But it seems like it's been on a journey. And there is a connection as I put this down, yourself I've got as a Christmas Tree. Now I like Christmas trees. There's something quite, I love the idea of having a tree, and the ceremony of it, and so on, and they're tall and statuesque, and a real presence to them. And respect for them, I think there's something about them, there is something I find about Christmas time and that kind of year. It may also be as it is coming around the corner as well. But in choosing that and when I saw this as our as our relationship I was a bit puzzled as to what would be in the middle here, a carrot, a basket of carrots so whatever is going on here, someone is selling these carrots and as I'm on my journey I'm buying this basket of carrots or something along the way. Does that make sense? I'm on my way home and I need some groceries, and you the tree are giving me some sort of, something tasty to take with me. So that's why I've chosen them. I've placed this one slightly up a hill, that maybe represent my tiredness today. It's the end of term and I can't wait for last few nights. So, it's probably more to do with me than anything else but there is something positive here as well, that's what I get from that. Does that make sense?
Brodie:	yes, it does.
DT:	how do you see it? Go on.
Brodie:	the one thing that I found really strange is that I didn't know what you had picked, but there was something about the tree, Christmas, and for some reason I thought oh I might pick one of them. But there wasn't, then you get the Christmas thing, and I thought about Christmas statuette, but there wasn't any. For the short time they stop it's like 'ok we can sit around the Christmas tree' they're not going to be shouting and fighting.
DT:	I agree with you there is something important about Christmas, for myself I find. I'm not sure my family stopped fighting around Christmas, but that is something else. But yeah, there's an importance to it at the end of the year. Funnily enough what I like about yours is you have this shaman here pointing the

way, and hippos are strange old things, funnily enough they kill more people in Africa than lions do.

Brodie: really?

DT: yeah, as they live in water a lot of the time, often when men come by on boats to fish or whatever else, they often stray into the hippos' territory without knowing, so then the hippo comes up and chomps through the boat or whatever else as they feel they're being threatened in some way. They don't mean it they don't hunt people down, it's just that they are quite territorial. But they are quite lovely.

Brodie: I don't know why, it just grabbed me.

DT: and the shaman. You do a lot of shamanic work do you?

Brodie: I just feel that it's something to do with, you know, I don't believe in these things, but I think that if I had a previously life, it must have been as a shaman. And I'm really intrigued in the paralleled between shamanism and psychotherapy. and the fact that shamans are, the real shamans, as I've done readings about it, are almost borderline personality disorders. And I have those traits, so you know

DT: lots of xxxx do

Brodie: so again, it's telling me I'm a shaman. It's the damage and whatever. And I like that, I don't know much, but I find it fascinating. And I really feel that in my work, that's

DT: transformation. I see what you mean.

Brodie: I don't know, I don't know.

DT: I can see it's quite strong.

Brodie: and with you, with the bear, I felt the strength and the sweetness and as I said it just came after I picked it, or after it came straight to me. Bears are a symbol of the mother, you know, so the mother looking after the cubs and um so I don't know, I have the sense that you, in your work or with your family with the people around you, in that sense you look after people, and you make sure that everything is fine. Again, I don't know where the other side is, the more aggressive part, and I don't know.

DT: well bears can be quite protective as well. I think both of them the bear and the hippo, they're very familial, they're strong and feminine both of them, as I understand it anyway. So yes, the bear can be very holding and nurturing of its cubs or whatever, and yet when threatened they're not necessarily hugely aggressive and they don't go out of their way to hunt. And when they track the salmon when they come up stream, they wait for hours, strangely. You're quite right. Shamans

	too in their work, are very patient, they watch the seasons, they watch the cycles.
Brodie:	don't know, they're not actually if you read about it, I don't know if you've read anything, they're not patient people.
DT:	really, is that true? My assumption totally
Brodie:	no, they're quite crazy, as I said they have proto borderline character traits, and they're very angry people, and you know, yeah, the original shaman. And it's funny because the original shamans are from the Russian, rather than American, as everyone believes.

Studying Dwight's Sand Tray

Turning to myself and exploring my own sort of projections on to my client, one of the things to note is that Catholicism, and therefore, religiousness, plays a massive role even on my side of the tray. My choice of a Christmas tree for Brodie suggests a projection onto him of something of my own religious identity, meaning he is religiously superior to myself, and is playing out my superego. To say a small amount more about my side, where there is a parallel process between myself and Brodie, is that we were both raised as Catholic. Yet, whereas whilst Brodie went to a Catholic school, I did not. My parents instead instilling within me from a very early age that power and worth were often tied to Catholicism and that should I ever step out of line, especially when I went to church, I would be punished. This is the hint of religious superiority which sits within all of us, as expressed briefly back in chapter two.

I even remember one particular instance whereby my younger brother and I were playing in church, semi-whispering as the congregation sang some hymn or another. At the end of the service though, our mother walked ahead of us on the way home saying nothing as she trudged up the road the five minutes from the parish church to our homestead. When she walked into the house, our mother said nothing to us, by which point I realised that there was something wrong. My mother went downstairs, picked up a belt, and came back upstairs to beat us for making 'too much noise' as she put it, in a church of the Lord and bringing shame upon her.

The importance of this should not be understated in that whilst I have marginally ignored religion as a cornerstone of supremacy, it is always important and is always present. Catholicism was part of the colonial narrative that was brought to Africa and transported to South America and was embedded within slaves, a process going back several hundreds of years. It has had a marked influence on how members of the LGBTQ community are treated within society as it has in regard as to how persons of colour were treated by their slave owners. The fact that things such as conversion therapy are often pitched within an overtly religious framework, shows just how powerful and insidious religion has become in assisting in the maintenance of supremacy. We only have to look at the number of religious wars fought around the globe to understand just how powerful a force religion becomes when influenced, nay infected with patriarchal, white supremacist, or capitalist narratives.

Summary

As we have considered the philosophy of supremacy, it is also worth returning to the internalised abuser on a collective level, not just an individual one. As stated in Chapter 3, one of the ideas I posited was that the internalised abuser in its creation of a fantasy idea of the other would use a form of psychological confirmation bias to confirm the said idea, thereby creating a self-contained loop of ideology, confirmation, and selfhood. One of the things to point out from that is how isolationist this internalised abuser actually is, be it individually or collectively.

The importance of returning to this topic for this chapter is that this is symptomatic of a collective experience as well as an individual one, whereby the lack of relationship between a collective subject group against the collective other is what can lead to fantasies about said other. This then forms in a similar fashion to the individual that collective internal group acts in a fashion whereby it seeks out material to confirm its biases, its sexism, its racism, its homophobia, and other means of oppression against the collective other. A perfect example on a collective level is the sheer number of stops and searches conducted within the United Kingdom and their disproportionate impact on minority groups (Various, 2021).

Whilst some of this will be down to crime in said area, given the collective nature of the culture conducting the searches, and of the education that those individuals within the services have received, the idea that there would not be some sort of individual and therefore collective bias, which therefore becomes a form of racism, is fairly flawed. It is always there, and it is only when we start to question how we have become internalised within supremacists' socially constructed systems that we then start to question how the internalised abuser that we have all got within ourselves may collectively oppress different groups outside of our own.

Supremacy, as I have continued to state, and will continue to do so, is a collective experience. Supremacy is not over there, it is not the fascists, it is not the communists, it is not even the capitalists. As Hannah Arendt (2018; Moyn, 2008) recognised in her excellent work, where she explores the banality of evil, what she actually recognised was supremacy sits within the individual and therefore the collective and how in its simplicity of action it can lead to the annihilation of millions.

The other factor to mention is to return to something touched on in Chapter 3, and it is the difference between an individual moral compass and a collective one. Often, when we engage within supremacist system, that collective moral compass is dictated to us by the collective superego at the pinnacle. We are defined and guided morally by something which is outside of ourselves, so all responsibility for any sort of guidance has gone. It is only when we start to individuate or recognise at the very least our tie to these forms of supremacy, that we then start to question and look to and take responsibility for our own morality and moral fortitude. Once we start to do that, only then do we then enter something more collectively moral, inclusive, and equitable.

This is the route to restructuring whole cultures, whereby inequality is maintained and there are people living on the streets, or in refuges, or there is not enough social care. That collective internal morality only comes with self-reflection and the acknowledgement of one's own collective abuser and one's own collective responsibility to tackle the self-destructive nature of ourselves.

Chapter Five of this book, therefore, looks at a possible route towards individually and collectively challenging the internalised supremacist. As we have seen, internalisations of the supremacist, or the activation of the supremacist wound, whilst embedded within all of us, may actually only emerge out of the difficult life experiences most of us encounter within our lives. So, for example, from the parentified child, who has been cast into the role of the caregiver for one's own parents via a route based around abuse or attachment trauma, and who then re-enacts that need to dominate, to judge and denigrate the good in others around them. Then there might be the culture which won the war, which, even though it suffered greatly for six years where men women, and children were traumatised and changed forever, managed to seemingly vanquish an evil to which its own royalty had ties, yet who decided they had a right to dominate and defile the cultural other, enforcing them to learn their own cultural lessons and embrace their own cultural shame, whilst not doing the same themselves.

The supremacist wound can be activated from a number of seemingly innocuous scenarios. This means that the failure to reflect and learn from the past and to engage with the individual and collective other from a humbler perspective, the failure to recognise the increased grandiosity of the subjugator, sits central to many of the ills committed by the patriarchy, by white supremacy and by capitalism. The sufferings of those of the gendered others, those who are white or non-white, the LGBTQ community, the class other, and even the planet, are then exacerbated by this pompous positioning of the Subject victorious over the numerous others around it.

References

Arendt, H. (2018). *The Human Condition* (2nd Editio). University of Chicago Press.
Bradway, K. (2006). What is sandplay? *Journal of Sandplay Therapy, 15*(2), 7–9.

Buber, M. (1952). *Eclipse of God*. Harper & Row Publishers Incorporated.
Buber, M. (2002). *Between Man and Man*. Routledge.
Buber, M. (2010). *I and Thou*. Martino Publishing Limited.
Butler, J. (1988). Performative acts and gender constitution: an essay in phenomenology and feminist theory. *Theatre Journal*, *40*(4), 519. 10.2307/3207893
Cox, M., & Thielgaard, A. (1986). *Mutative Metaphors in Psychotherapy: The Aeolian Mode*. Tavistock.
Deleuze, G., & Guattari, F. (2013). *A Thousand Plateaus*. Bloomsbury Academic.
Delmas, M. A., & Burbano, V. C. (2011). The drivers of greenwashing. *California Management Review*, *54*(1), 64–87. 10.1525/cmr.2011.54.1.64
Diangelo, R. (2018). *White Fragility: Why It's So Hard for White People to Talk About Racism*. Beacon Press.
Dudley, M. Q. (2017). A library matter of genocide: the library of congress and the historiography of the Native American Holocaust. *International Indigenous Policy Journal*, *8*(2). 10.18584/iipj.2017.8.2.9
Hand, S. (2009). *Emmanuel Levinas (Routledge Critical Thinkers)* (Vol. 53, Issue 1). Routledge. 10.1111/j.1468-2265.2011.00689.x
Jacobs, M. (2003). *Sigmund Freud - Key figures in Counselling and Psychotherapy* (2nd ed.). Sage Publications.
Jakimowicz, S., Perry, L., & Lewis, J. (2021). Bowen family systems theory: mapping a framework to support critical care nurses' well-being and care quality. *Nursing Philosophy*, *22*(2). 10.1111/nup.12320
James, S. (2014). *Spinoza on Philosophy, Religion, and Politics: The Theologico-Political Treatise*. Oxford University Press.
Johnson, R. A. (1993). *Owning Your Own Shadow: Understanding the Dark Side of the Psyche*. Harper Collins Publishers.
Jones, S. (2006). Antonio Gramsci. In *Routledge Critical Thinkers*. Routledge. 10.4324/9780203625521
Jung, C. G. (1990). *The Undiscovered Self*. Princeton University Press.
Kirschner, S. R. (2012). How not to other the other (and similarly impossible goals): scenes from a psychoanalytic clinic and an inclusive classroom. *Journal of Theoretical and Philosophical Psychology*, *32*(4), 214–229. 10.1037/a0030158
Labovitz Boik, B., & Anna Goodwin, E. (2000). *Sandplay Therapy A Step-by-Step Manual For Psychotherapists of Diverse Orientations*. W. W. Norton and Company.
Levinas, E. (2006). *Humanism of the Other*. University of Illinois Press.
Markham, D., Khare, A., & Beckman, T. (2014). Greenwashing: a proposal to restrict its spread. *Journal of Environmental Assessment Policy and Management*, *16*(4), 1–16. 10.1142/S1464333214500306
Mason, C. (2022). *Partygate Fines: Are Boris Johnson and Rishi Sunak finished?* BBC News Online. https://www.bbc.co.uk/news/uk-politics-61079172
Moyn, S. (2008). Hannah Arendt on the secular. *New German Critique*, *35*(3), 71–96. 10.1215/0094033X-2008-014
Proctor, G. (2010). Boundaries or mutuality in therapy: is mutuality really possible or is therapy doomed from the start? *Psychotherapy and Politics International*, *8*(1), 44–58. 10.1002/ppi
Ram, M. (2014). White but not quite: normalizing colonial conquests through spatial mimicry. *Antipode*, *46*(3), 736–753. 10.1111/anti.12071

Romanyshyn, R. D. (2010). *The Wounded Researcher: Making a Place for Unconscious Dynamics in the Research Process. December 2013*, 37–41. 10.1080/08873267.2010.523282

Rousseau, J.-J. (1984). *A Discourse on Inequality*. Penguin Books Limited.

Sartre, J.-P., & MacCombie, J. (1964). Jean-Paul Sartre black orpheus. *The Massachusetts Review, Inc, 6*(1), 13–52. http://www.jstor.org/stable/25087216

Sletvold, J. (2013). The ego and the id revisited Freud and Damasio on the body ego/ self. *The International Journal of Psycho-Analysis, 94*(5), 1019–1032. 10.1111/1745-8315.12097

Spinoza, B. (1996). *Ethics*. Penguin Classics.

Turner, B. A. (2005). *The Handbook of Sandplay Therapy*. Tenemos Press.

Turner, D. (2016). Examining Buber's I: narcissism and the othering of the other. *Journal of Critical Psychology Counselling and Psychotherapy, 16*(June), 113–117.

Various (2013). *Engaging with Climate Change: Psychoanalytic and Interdisciplinary Perspectives* (S. Weintrobe (Ed.)). Routledge.

Various (2014). *#TBT: When The Advocate Invented Bears*. The Advocate. https://www.advocate.com/comedy/2014/04/17/tbt-when-advocate-invented-bears

Various (2020). *Schools and COVID-19: guidance for Black, Asian and minority ethnic (BAME) staff and their employers in school settings*. https://www.fom.ac.uk/covid-19/update-risk-reduction-framework-for-nhs-staff-at-risk-of-covid-19-

Various (2021). *Ethnicity Facts and Figures: Stop and Search Statistics*. GOV.UK. https://www.ethnicity-facts-figures.service.gov.uk/crime-justice-and-the-law/policing/stop-and-search/latest#by-ethnicity

von Franz, M.-L. (1980). *Projection and Re-Collection in Jungian Psychology*. Open Court Publications.

Winnicott, D. W. (1969). *The Use of an Object*. 711–716.

Woskie, L., & Wenham, C. (2021). Do men and women "lockdown" differently? examining Panama's covid-19 sex-segregated social distancing policy. *Feminist Economics, 0*(0), 1–18. 10.1080/13545701.2020.1867761

Zimmerman, L. (2020). *Trauma and the Discourse of Climate Change: Literature, Psychoanalysis and Denial Paperback – 13 April 2020*. Routledge.

Chapter 5

Activism and Supremacy

By the spring of 1942, Operation Barbosa, the German invasion of the Soviet Union, had more or less failed. Even though the Germans held a good deal of territory, including huge swathes of Ukraine, Belarus, and the Baltic Republics, they had not yet conquered the Soviet Union to a point where it stood still. The culmination of this attempt by the Germans to complete their war on the Eastern front involved the Battle of Stalingrad which ran from August 1942 to February 1943. This battle was seen as one of the bloodiest battles in the history of warfare and with an estimated two million casualties. Today, this battle is considered one of the major turning points, not just in the German conflict along the Eastern front, but within the whole of World War II. The Soviet Union's ultimate victory at Stalingrad motivated the Red Army to such an extent that it changed the direction of the whole war, and the Germans were finally pushed back toward Berlin where they were ultimately conquered in 1945 (Beevor, 1999).

This immense battle, these events which cost millions of Soviet lives, could be seen as an enormous cultural scar upon the psyche of the Soviet Union. The subsequent years evolved into the Cold War, where a good number of nations were formed into an Easter Block, a block designed to protect the Soviet Union from NATO and the forces of the West, and a block whose dividing line actually involved the splitting in two of Germany and the symbolic introduction of the Berlin Wall (Westad, 2018).

For those who do not know, as a former member of the Royal Air Force, I had the pleasure of serving some of my time in Berlin, albeit at the very end of the Cold War. Berlin, during my time there, was a city very much divided in two. Most notable was that given that West Berlin was the scene of what many might term capitalist opulence, with numerous high-end shops, cafes, expensive homes, the residences in the former East of Berlin were often characterised by the grey, high-rise buildings which often littered the skyline. Across both halves of Berlin though, there was always an underclass, a class of immigrants on both sides of this Cold War divide, an underclass which frequented some of the more regular pubs, bars, and clubs which were situated in such a beautiful city. Berlin was a symbol, if you like, of the mistrust

DOI: 10.4324/9781003313229-5

of the Soviet Union should anything like the invasion of its country happen again. It was a scar that, even with the de-Nazification of Germany post the Second World War, would reside within the Soviet psyche ever since said trauma (Coates, 2014).

In some ways, it is no surprise that in February of 2022, Vladimir Putin unilaterally decided to invade Ukraine. His reasoning was that there was a rising Nazi tide in Ukraine and that it needed to be stamped out. At the time of writing this book, whilst I cannot say if Putin was right about Nazism in Ukraine, what I can suggest is there is an enormous cultural projection of something fearful onto Ukraine and the Ukrainians, as well as NATO itself. This fear has led to anger at the invasion, and at the war crimes, allegedly, committed by Russian troops. It has brought home for many in the West just how fragile their existence actually is when news reports have often pointed out this strange presumption that war does not happen in the West, whilst looking straight down the metaphorical barrel of a war conducted mere hours flying time away from their safe, comfortable, dissociated homes (Alyukov, 2022; Haukkala, 2015).

The purpose of this chapter though is not to offer a diatribe around war and conflict. It is, though to point out that in this last stage of understanding supremacy, one of the ways in which supremacy repopulates itself is through trauma. Cultural trauma of the type endured by the Soviet nation in the Second World War is something which is probably unfathomable to understand. It is an event discussed I am sure in the schools and expressed by the elders within the said culture. This war, this anger, this attempt at the destruction of so many, will sit deep within the psyche of their culture. In a similar vein, on the Western Front, where the United Kingdom and the United States of America often aggrandise their contribution to the war effort, there is an avoidance of the impact of six years of global conflict upon the collective cultural psyche.

Again, the failure to acknowledge that war involves trauma through the dehumanisation of another means that it is irrelevant who the winner or the loser is because both parties in that attempt to take the life of another have become dehumanised in the said process (Luna, 2015). Their sense of self, their sense of who they are, their sense of their humanity, will always be changed in a process of war, be they service persons serving on the front line, or family members left at home waiting to hear from loved ones sent to conflict, or elders or youngers who are sent out from their homes to exist in the relative safety of the countryside as was such during the Second World War.

War involves an enormous psychological adaption to a process of existential angst and fear. It is not a normal, if I may use this word, place to reside within. It is a distortion of anything peaceful, of anything restful, of anything relatively boring about human existence and we underestimate its impact upon us all. Of the times that I know of where a whole country has been encouraged to look at its engagement with conflict, such as the aforementioned de-Nazification of Germany, these are the only occasions when a whole culture has had to take a strong, powerful look at itself and re-evaluate its own cultural principles accordingly. This is not to say that these processes have been perfect, that because Germany has gone through a de-Nazification programme instituted by the powers of the West and the East that it is therefore clean and clear of a fascist influence. Supremacy, by its very nature, is insidious and unconscious and, in an increasingly globalised world, will always re-populate itself, like the many-headed hydra of mythology where, should you cut off one head, three will replace it. War, by its nature, is a horror, and activism. An activism whereby we stand up for the rights of the many when driven by a need to do what is right, can often be a form of personal or collective conflict that can feel as traumatic, as tiring, as exhausting as going to war (Proctor, 2010).

This chapter will therefore explore activism; first of all, looking at psychotherapy as a form of activism before considering the psychopathology of the activist including consideration of the distortions within the activist when there is an unresolved trauma. This chapter will then explore the archetype of the activist, as I see it, before looking at the process of decolonisation, a term often used in popular culture, but from within a psychotherapeutic framework a term which is as often misunderstood.

The first part of this process though involves an exploration of psychotherapy and activism.

Psychotherapy as Activism

A colleague of mine many years ago said to me that he did not believe that psychotherapy was political and that for him, he always fought to maintain a separation between his psychotherapy practice and the culture wars. This sort of idea is actually fairly common within counselling and psychotherapy in the global north. The idea that as therapists we should be apolitical, sort of creates the narrative that we should not hold a political position whilst in the therapeutic space with our clients. As this book has already expressed, if we are all impacted by views and visions which may lead us to be either more empathetic; to offer tokenistic gestures to persons of colour; to perhaps engage from a more sort of right wing perspective, or left wing; to be perhaps more homophobic than we like to admit, the reality is that even unconsciously those narratives will enter the psychotherapeutic frame with our clients of difference, no matter which intersectional identity they, or we, are. Psychotherapy in those instances is always impacted by the political constructs that we have engaged within in order to form a sense of our identity (D. D. L. Turner, 2022).

As both therapist and client are already impacted and moulded by the political it is therefore impossible for a therapist to be totally apolitical. They may believe that because they do not vote in an election that therefore they are not political, but what they fail to recognise is that when they were growing up, they would have been informed by the political narratives passed down by their parents, through society. These would have informed who they were supposed to be and how they were supposed to act as a man, a woman, or another.

From, firstly, the client of mine, that I saw many years ago and who was raised in a time pre the abolition of laws outlawing homosexuality and was a trainee on a training course in counselling where he told me a story about having to sit with a client who was clearly homophobic. To, secondly, the supervisee, from a middle class background, sat with a young woman from a working class background who was expressing their distress at rising fuel prices across the global north, and was then met with disdain by said middle-class therapist; a dismissal of her own unique experience which then led to her refusing to re-engage with the therapist accordingly. These briefest of examples show that the political is actually always present within the world of psychotherapy.

So, for the colleague who chose to narrate the idea that in his practice the political had no place, for many of those hindered or impacted by political decisions designed to exclude or marginalise, their experiences will always be doubly difficult. In a capitalist society, the number of times I have students of difference (and not necessarily just of colour, more often I should add of class), who express that they would like to train but that the courses they are applying to offer no bursaries, no subsidies, no assistance, so therefore it is impossible for them to pay the tens of thousands of pounds for a two to four-year course, is extraordinary and should not, in this current day and age, still occur.

One of the other reasons why I state that therapy by its very nature is political, is that often in the work that we do with our clients, we end up having to hold projections. When I say projections plural, what I mean is that projection as it is posited is not just one aspect of the client that they are unwilling to own, it is multiple facets, multiple aspects of a client's identity which they have struggled to integrate or re-integrate and which they have distanced themselves from. These projections, which have often been generated in early life contexts, will also often have a political component intertwined within them. To say a little bit more about what I mean here, it is best to actually explore what a projection actually is.

A projection in psychodynamic terms, involves the splitting off and casting out of that which is deemed to be unnecessary, unworthy, or undesirable by the ego (Vaillant, 1994; von Franz, 1980). Often a process which has been encouraged through the superego, it is something which can be enforced via the cultural rules of the day. So for example, in an earlier chapter when I explored the client who felt unable to express her anger out of a fear of being labelled as angry or hysterical, as previously stated and it is worth re-stating here, that idea that a woman should not be angry was emergent out of the patriarchal system which said a woman should act in a certain fashion to complement a man and in this case not to be angry.

That idea would have been reinforced through the laws of our time, through the mental health services within which numerous women have been misdiagnosed, and via other cultural and religious edicts and structures (Freud, 2014; Mitchell, 1986).

The next part to actually explore here is actually around the idea of defences (Perry & Bond, 2017). Every client who ever enters a psychotherapeutic space will enter willingly, that is without a doubt. Yet, what will also come with them is every defence, every structure they have built around themselves in order to survive until the point of entering therapy. These psychological defences could be anything from denial, to repression, to reaction formation, to a flight to health (Vaillant, 1994). Defences are a necessary part of the egoic structure and actually in many ways protect one's egoic sense of self from the shadow or that which has been repressed and has been projected outwards onto another. One defence in particular though, I think works well within this realm of socially constructed forms of identity and that is of deflection. The idea of deflection, was initially posited out of the world of psychodynamic psychotherapy (Freud, 2014; Perry & Bond, 2017). This idea involves the recognition of that which is being repressed within one's own egoic sense of self, but which is then, instead of being used against the systemic part of the superego, will then be pushed to one side onto a lesser, more amenable object for said projection.

Displacement here in many ways then becomes an avoidance of focusing one's attention against that which has either upset or moved us in some way. For example, when we avoid the object of our affection and supply love and attention to something or someone else, be they human, animal, or environmental as a way of avoiding feeling let down, sad or even loved by another closer to us. Displacement is a common factor in relationships with the other. As already expressed early on in Chapter 2, in the example with where the client displaced a lot of her upset and anger at being left by her previous therapist onto myself, displacement is not just a conscious thing it is an unconscious process. In that client's case, the fact that she had taken something that she unconsciously knew and displaced it upon myself, was particularly of interest. In fact, it is not uncommon, as Adey (2020) pointed out, that when it comes to our prejudices often what happens is we either displace or that we are politically encouraged to displace emotions, feelings, etc onto another beyond our core group. Offering a broader example out of the culture, displacement is something which was very much central to the Brexit vote, whereby an external other was created and therefore emotions of hatred, anger, and fear were displaced upon a group which was never actually a threat to ourselves. The maintenance of supremacy, therefore, involves the manipulation of a narrative by the central force which is then passed through the acolytes and used against the other.

The other part of this is actually splitting. Splitting is an idea which is posited by psychodynamic theorists such as Melanie Klein (Mitchell, 1986) who saw splitting as a core facet of coming into life whereby we split off much of our potential about who we are in order to conform to certain ways and ideals of being as laid out by our family, gender, our group or any other sort of system. Splitting therefore involves the repression of that potential. When we consider the drive towards supremacy and the external supremacist aspect of the superego, what we often have to recognise is that in that move away from one's own moral core, there has to be a splitting off of that aspect of who we are, that connection to something more real, authentic and moralistically driven, to then adhere to a socially constructed super egoic sense of what is morally right and wrong for us as individuals and as a collective.

So, when we discussed the supremacy complex, deflection and splitting become core facets of the process of creating another other. As I have stated, we have seen this used in political spheres and is often a tool used by the political right who will marginalise an other group in order to bolster the position of their own said group. A recent example in the United Kingdom is emergent from the failure of the Conservative Party of the current time to adhere to a policy in their political manifesto whereby they would ban conversion therapy within the LGBTQ community. This ban, when it was finally instituted, had changed to one where it involves the splitting of a whole community into two, meaning that on a practical level, only those who identified as LGB were a part of the banning of conversion therapy. On the opposite side of this divide, those who identified as Trans were not proffered the same level of support and safety. They had become the projected other.

This divide and rule system, this deflection and splitting as we see here, involves the creation of a third out group whereby all fears of otherness are placed upon them unnecessarily and unfairly. Yet, what it also does is it co-opts the power and the strength of the LGB community and brings them more onside, bringing them into the space where they are potentially acolytes for the patriarchal, white supremacist, heteronormative ideal at the centre. The impact of this split and of this deflection, is the increased levels of fear and sadness and anger at their treatment by authorities of those who identify as Trans thereby exacerbating difficult experiences of otherness which already sit within this community (Bachmann & Gooch, 2017).

Deflection and splitting are not new types of socially and politically motivated defences though. These have been used for generations to split families and groups and create forms of others who need to be marginalised, contained, or destroyed. Yet, what it also does is galvanises an out group to continue to fight for their rights to be accepted and seen as human beings. The recent political movement to send illegal refugees who arrive in the United Kingdom to Rwanda is another example of this deflection and projection (Enver, 2022). Again, a political narrative formed within the United Kingdom, the idea is actually that it is only those who are men who are sent away from the United Kingdom, suggesting that those who are women or children or who are on the other side of that familial coin, would be allowed to enter as refugees.

It should also be noted that this split has happened in other areas, such as within the internment camps on the Isle of Man for German/Austrian sympathisers during the Second World War, and in America where camps were used to contain seemingly Japanese sympathisers during World War II, post Pearl Harbour (Unknown, 2016). It is also something which has been used a lot during slavery, where the split between the house Negro and the field Negro built up a conflict between both parties, one which sits within the racial framework to this day and, as previously stated, is something which has sat in the colonised psyche of the Scottish and the Irish, post their horrific treatment during times of colonialism (Akbar, 1984; Valdés Miyares, 2017).

The transgenerational impact of these splits and deflections combined should therefore not be underestimated when working with our clients. The idea, therefore, that psychotherapists are working within the political arena, therefore, arises in part out of the factor that all our identities, the projections and the deflections either conducted or held have arisen out of the political landscape which moulds us all. This, therefore, means that in the work that we do, the drive to help and assist our clients to become more fully who they are and to re-integrate these aspects of themselves, and to recognise the projections and deflections, is a political act. This is where I will borrow the Jungian term 'individuation', noting that individuation, when seen through a social constructionist lens, actually also involves the political (Stein, 2005). This individuating process involves the stripping back of the political internalisations of identity to then become truer to oneself beyond those said political structures which have formed the sense of who we are.

Whilst writing this book, I cannot presume to believe that Carl Jung meant to see individuation as a political act, but what I can say clearly is that as much as it is psychological that individuation is also strongly sociological and therefore political. What we as practitioners failed to recognise in that socially constructed vision of what politics actually is, is that the political sphere has always had an influence not just on our work but in a far more nuanced and far-reaching way upon who we are as individuals and as collectives. So, therefore when I talk about the importance of individuating our clients, what we are doing is that we are engaging with the political within ourselves. Individuation is therefore an act of psychological activism against the tyranny of the socially constructed aspects of the psyche.

Psychotherapy brings humanity, realness, and compassion to those parts which have been marginalised and denied when the psychological order was first struck (Lacan, 2003). This exploration of the union between psychotherapy, the psychological, and activism, and its pros and cons, is explored within the next section.

The Psychopathology of the Activist

In considering activism and how psychotherapy is actually a form of activism, it is important though to recognise where there is a major difference between activism driven by one's own unresolved psychology and activism which comes from a place of an internal moral dialogue with one's own shadow self. This section will therefore expand on this particular idea as much as possible, offering one or two examples of where this might occur.

Some of the background for this particular section arises from the works of Jessica Benjamin (1998) and Judith Butler (1997) who speak a fair amount about how an overidentification with a sense of otherness can also be seen as narcissistic. Yet, my attempt here is to tie this together with Butler's work or understanding activism, whereby she picks out certain instances in some of her writing of activists who, in their drive to be seen as correct, have maybe inadvertently, maybe not, oppressed others. As a consequence, this drive being driven their own trauma.

The Trauma Driven Activist

Trauma is a major factor within the activist's inner dialogue with themselves. It is often down to an activist to take up the reigns and the fight for equality. In the work of the likes of van der Kolk (2015), there is a recognition that unresolved trauma can often become something shadowy within the psyche which is then projected out onto the other. This is the meaning behind the image Figure 5.1. As the diagram states quite clearly, trauma driven activism is also narcissistic and othering of the other. The trauma driven activist, whilst initially well-meaning, may use their own capitalist, or gendered, or

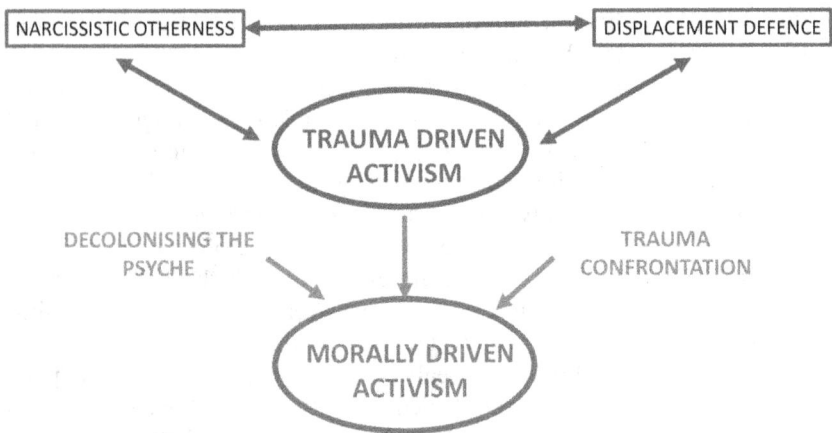

Figure 5.1 The Psychology of Activism.

racialised power to enforce their own doctrine and ideals upon the other. Examples of this are many and frequent in society today and, for example, some of the anti-trans dialogue, which is apparent in society, is often posited as coming from a space of feminist activism. Whilst for some this may well be correct, there will also be those for whom this unresolved trauma around patriarchal superiority has then fed into their own narrative around a different minority group.

The importance here is not to silence the trauma driven activist, but it is to encourage those individuals and those groups to consider their own wounding before taking up such a position of superiority. In some ways, this superiority defence as discussed earlier on, also sits within the trauma driven activist. The need to maintain a sense of othering and other is a core component of the trauma driven activist which then leaves that person outside of a relationship with the other they are so fearful of.

Another core facet of this form of activism is that it is not intersectional. It has struggled to take into consideration its own superiority, its own inbred positioning, its own inbred white supremacist, patriarch, or capitalist. This failure then means that whilst the trauma driven activist may use their power, be it financial or racial power, to affect some kind of rescued distancing from the threat of a particular other group, what they are actually doing is harking back to the comfort of those internalised systems of socially constructed superiority. This is no different when considered from a racialised perspective.

Offering a perhaps surprising example, Martin Luther King, whilst considered to this day a major advocate for civil rights, was a part of a group who were uncomfortable with the sexuality of their contemporary James Baldwin, whose intersectional identities as a black gay man did not align with King's religious perspective on sexuality identity (Campbell, 2021). So that whereas in the early stages of their work together, Baldwin felt included in the dialogues around race and difference, by the end of King's life, pre-his assassination, Baldwin had been very much side-lined from the fight for racial justice in America. This example here actually shows in King's case, that whilst he was undoubtedly a great man, and whilst he did undoubtedly fight against white supremacy, he too had taken up a position of patriarchal and an also religious superiority over another vocal activist and man of colour, purely because of his sexuality.

That we all, as activists, no matter what our position, need to work through these intersectional mazes, is a massive factor for us as we walk towards some form of individuation from the social constructions of identity within which we are embedded. The trauma driven activist, whilst presenting as well-meaning will always still have psychological work to do to achieve their goal of internal and external equality. Equality is not just an external ideal is what I am saying here. It is something which Lacan recognised needed to happen in the relationship between the egoic sense of self and the shadow or the unconscious, as much as it is between those disparate groups which sit outside and walk amongst us (Homer, 2007).

For the trauma driven activist, much of the activism though is about the destruction of that which is external, the burning down of those socially constructed structures which dominate us all. Whilst at the same time not altering or changing anything within ourselves accordingly. Another major issue with this desire to burn it all down, to topple the statues, to rid ourselves of the past or to change the present, is that if the other is the shadow, then all our egoic sense of self, therefore our narcissistic sense of self, is trying to do is to actually destroy that which makes us unique. To destroy, to burn down, to take away from is actually no less an attempt to destroy, to marginalise, and to denigrate that which makes us who we are ultimately.

What I ultimately mean though, is that for the trauma driven activist, they are very much driven by the displacement and the splitting and the projection of their own feelings and aspects of their own internalised traumatic self onto objects and others accordingly. The need to destroy, the need to ruin and get rid of said structures is actually nothing more than an attempt to destroy and rid themselves of that which is unconsciously within them trying to be known and reintegrated. An avoidance of this type of internalised pain is often what drives the trauma driven activist, but even that is projected outwards. The idea that one can protect huge swathes of people from pain can often become a massive internal goal (echoing the statement that no-one should feel the same way that I felt when I went through this, for example). Yet, whilst this is admirable in certain ways, what it also does is avoid the fact that actually that pain for some of us, especially for those of us who have been on the receiving end, has moved us and has created who we are right here, right now.

This is not to say that we have to leave those in suffering to continue to suffer in some way, as that is nonsense, but it is to say that I am not so omnipotent that I can ever save huge swathes of the population from en-during any sort of suffering at all. I can make the world a marginally better place by doing the work that I need to do, that we all need to do in order to face up to who we actually are. A combination of both good and evil, of both righteousness and cruelty.

Supervisee Sam was a trainee counsellor on the third year of his course. From a working-class background, he was bullied by his siblings and peers at school, his reason for ultimately becoming a counsellor being one where he wanted to fight for the rights of the other, especially the working class. His client, Rachel, saw him for six sessions of short-term work around the breakup of a relationship, where her ex-partner had left her by cheating with another woman. In the very last session though, Rachel, stated that it was her birthday, and she would be having a party in a local bar. She invited Sam to go along. Sam did not take the dilemma to supervision, and instead decided to go to the party, where he was asked by several people what he did and how he knew Rachel (he acknowledged that he was her therapist). During group supervision, a number of the women in the group questioned Sam's desire to go to the party and were quite critical of his reasons for breaking some obvious boundaries in counselling and psychotherapy. During the following session though, Sam returned in angry at the supervisor for not protecting him from rest of the group. He felt they had been extremely unkind towards him, had spoken to him harshly, their behaviour, he stated, being not at all in line with the modality they were all a part of. Sam left the group at that point.

Using this example of Sam, what he has done is take umbrage at having to recognise his own abusive side, the side which led to him acting out an obvious erotic transference with his client (Rouholamin, 2007). The rest of the supervision group though picked up on this and were left understandably unsettled by what they had heard, together with Sam's inabilities to both recognise what he had done and his ability to express what he had done so confidently. One of the most interesting points though is in Sam's scrabbling for the victim position he attempted to distance himself from the abuser, projecting this onto his supervisor. He needed to be seen as a good man who had done no wrong.

This singular unconscious engagement, and then conscious disengagement with his own power can often be replicated on a collective level. In these societal situations what we often actually start to see is that this projection of the abuser onto a totality is an aspect of the trauma driven activist which needs to be owned and re-integrated. As discussed in Chapter Two, the fact that one is a civil rights activist, or a feminist, or a disability activist, does not prevent one from acting out one's homophobia, racism, or sexism; we are all formed from the triumvirate of supremacys, they all act out unconsciously within us. This narcissistic need to be seen as 'good' all the time, and the failure to recognise that one is built to be also 'bad' means that the pain or acknowledging one's own evil is displaced outwards onto another, often unwitting, other (Benjamin, 1998; Kristeva, 1994).

Alongside this, though there can also be the mass projection of the victim onto those who could potentially become victims were the abuser left unchecked. In extreme cases, this total vision of a whole group of minorities as being victims or potential victims, whilst a helpful start point, can actually become really quite disempowering for those other individuals. But the most important part of all of this is to recognise the over-identification of the trauma driven activist with their own need to rescue. The white saviour complex is a perfect example of this.

In some ways tied to ideas about complexes, and therefore in this instance, the superiority complex, what I am actually saying here is that this split is detrimental in the othering of both victims and abusers en masse alike and the over-identification with the rescuer or hero archetype for that person sat in the middle. This is not to say that good work cannot be done from this position, as it can, but it also has to be done with a sense of self-awareness that one is not going to be able to save everybody, that one is not going to be able to fix the whole world's problems within one's lifetime. Patriarchy for example, as previously stated is tens of thousands of years old. So, any belief that one will change things today, now, within this lifetime, is flawed to failure from its inception. This movement, this idea, this ideal has underlying it the narcissistic need for immediate satisfaction. In extreme cases, where I have watched activists, many of whom are not just psychotherapists and counsellors, work themselves to the bone, their levels of self-care have really been quite poor, for example. They have abused themselves in their self-neglect.

The reason I mention this is that this desire, this need to be the person out there at forefront of a movement, who is saving the world from the world, can often drive an individual beyond their own limits, boundaries, and levels of personal safety. So, whilst the projected abuser sits outside of oneself and needs to be confronted, what can often happen for this type of activist is that they become quite self-abusive in the drive to attain the goal of equality and equity.

Morally Driven Activist

Therefore, to move from this position as a trauma driven activist to one where we are more morally driven and where our activism is not informed by our trauma, is where we need to go. This does not mean that our trauma is healed; this does not mean that it does not on occasion take us over, and our inner traumatised children run riot and create havoc. What it does mean is that those internalised socially constructed structures which have left us perhaps traumatised are therefore seen, acknowledged, and contained in a way that perhaps they have not been before. Also, morality here, for the morally driven activist which is the antithesis of the aforementioned trauma driven activist, is something which arises from deep within the unconscious, the self or the spiritual (the reader may take whichever term they wish to use and apply it to themself). A morally driven activist has worked hard to de-colonise their own psyche, to challenge their internalised patriarchal sense of self and to look at how their own complicity with capitalism and the money states have led to the oppressions of many others around the world.

This is not through the stretching to be an ideal. This involves a constant recognition of how one's self, one's identity, one's creativity, one's dress code, one's attitudes, one's words, one's ability to relate to others, one's ability to hold relationships, how all these and many other facets of day to day living, and day to day being a human being, have been colonised by the western powers. We see how these have been changed by ideas about how we are supposed to be as a man or a woman, have been tempered by how we are supposed to be around our sexuality, and how they may have been changed based around how society views our neuro-ability, disability, or class, or age, or race. The importance of this ongoing constant refinement is that we edge inexorably towards an internal sense of who we are as a decolonised sense of self.

Yet, in doing so, what the morally driven activist also has to do is confront their own trauma. What one means by this is that any experience, as I have previously stated, becomes internalised. Not just the positive ones. For the person who has been abused, or the person who has been neglected, rejected, abandoned, that entity, that symbol, that system will become a part of the person's psychology. This book has offered a number of examples of where the internalisation of a systemic narrative has led either to their silencing, their inability to speak up, their fear of being seen as aggressive in racially dominant spaces, or their need to hide aspects of their intersectional identity out of a fear that those parts will not be respected, seen, and held.

Yet even though those examples are often driven by a type of external truth, what there often also is, is an unconscious super-egoic angle which drives the narrative anyway. So, for example, for those students or therapists who find it difficult to find their own voice in say patriarchal spaces, or white spaces, or ableist spaces, or spaces where there are elders, one of the messages they may have internalised, is that one has to keep quiet -because the adults, those who are white, the men, those who are able-bodied, those who are older, are speaking. This may not be an overt message, although sometimes it is. What it may be is that actually one has learned this through the constant, often unconscious re-affirming of a sense of superiority of the centre, when in centre-led spaces.

To offer an example from my own experience, I remember that at a meeting speaking on issues of equality, diversity, and inclusion I was told by a person in said meeting that I should 'watch my tone'. Tone policing is a massive part of the experience of the other and comes out of a supremacist narrative of 'You must know your place when you speak to me as I am your superior'. What it also can do, when repeated or implied, is leave oneself feeling silenced, unheard, and invisible. Now, in my particular case, I chose to carry on speaking anyway, but that is because I had done the work to maintain my voice and to give it free expression. In some ways, that is the reason for this book, that is the reason for the blogs that I write, the papers, the chapters, the speeches, the presentations, and the rants on Twitter. They give my voice expression. Yet, for many others that is not a possibility.

For the morally driven activist, there is also a recognition that the goal they are attempting to attain is not one that will be held in their lifetime. This is an aspect of the morally driven activist which recognises that they are not the totality of experience, that they are not as morally superior as Superman. The morally driven activist knows that in order for this to work two things have to happen:

1 Firstly, they have to work in communication and relationship with other activists on similar paths to themselves, not necessarily the same ones because that is almost impossible

2   The second part is to remember their own humanity and to recognise that without the support of friends, family, or those closest to them in whatever way, shape, or form they will burn out, their self-care will suffer and that they will become useless to anyone who might be in need of their assistance

This second aspect holds echoes of the work of Gilligan, and her understanding of the ethics of care (Gilligan, 2014). An idea is emergent out of a patriarchal study into scales of care and morality, Gilligan recognised that for women, care and the decisions one might make based around a series of ethical questions, was not something to be assessed purely through a white patriarchal lens. Care for women, she argued, was more relational, and therefore less individualistic, than it might be for men.

Although this is a contested subject, with some theorists struggling to define what care actually is, my view here is that some of these negative perspectives take away from the phenomenological opening Gilligan's idea recognises (Held, 2014). To propose that care can be rationally defined is by its very nature an idea rooted in the supremacy of patriarchy and white supremacy. These ideas ignore that care in indigenous communities is a very different beast, whilst then failing to see that care is universal, and in many ways archetypal. It is an experience, a feeling, and a desire to help others (Bookman & Aboulafia, 2000). There is a depth of care which stretches beyond and challenges the singular strictures enforced from within the superego informed triad of supremacy.

A dream that I had recently emphasised this:

The dream involved my walking up a hill with a friend whose funeral I had just attended that same day. As I walked up the hill, this friend pointed out the plots for 17 trees that he realised that he said that I had planted on my previous visit there. In the dream, I had no recollection of having done so, but I appreciated him reminding me of my experience there. We passed by some stalls along the way, looking for things to buy, things to purchase before picking up one or two small items, an umbrella to keep the sun off and a bottle of water. We walked back to where the trees were and he said to me, 'You'll be long gone by the time you sit in their shade' and then we walked back down the hill together, which is where the dream ended.

This dream was actually on the night after the funeral of a friend, but it was a friend who understood the work that I have to do as an activist and as a psychotherapist. The dream holds echoes of a famous saying which goes something along the lines of 'He who plants a tree knowing that he will never sit in its shade understands the meaning of life'. The fact that this scene, this gift emerged on the night of a funeral and has stayed with me for so long is, in my view, an expression of that morally given part, that unconscious part that knows the work I have to do but recognises that I cannot do it alone. It recognises that it is a long journey, that I will be long departed from this mortal plain and be back with the ancestors by the time this mission is anywhere near its completion.

The morally driven activist is therefore aware of the split within its own psyche and has engaged in a process of self-reflection and therefore self-discovery in order to re-discover and re-place that which had been split off in its attempts to come into being and its compliance with society. The morally driven activist is not perfect by any means; this is not what this is ultimately about. The morally driven activist is very much aware of their own flaws and their inaccuracies. It is aware of the shame of the things that it has done in order to get to this point. It is aware of where it has complied, performed, oppressed, beaten, cajoled, has repressed its own sense of morality, in order to act out in some way and impact someone else or some other group. It is aware of its own trauma and the pain that it has been left with over a period of time, a pain which in an attempt to avoid and displace said pain has been therefore projected outwards onto numerous individuals and other groups.

The split between the morally driven activist and its own morality becomes aligned and reconnected through the inner work of decolonising one's own self from the impacts of the external supremacist triad. The morally driven activist is not so much driven by a higher power, it is driven by something inward and unconscious. In fact, if I change my wording then what I actually mean is that the morally driven activist is guided by an unconscious yet very powerful hand.

So, for the morally driven activist, understanding their sense of otherness and giving it some free rein, working out how that sense of otherness is being silenced, has been oppressed or hidden, and uncovering the internalised supremacist or abuser becomes a core tenet towards working intersectionally. This can be done through personal exploration, through working with certain therapists who are politically driven, and there are a growing number out there who have taken up the reins. Or it can be done heuristically, where one explores one's own processes around difference and otherness and looks to understand the internalised supremacist and sense of otherness and how they may often joust for political position and superiority within the unconsciousness of the psyche. To understand the notion of the morally driven activist though, one has to recognise that the activist is actually an archetype, an archetype that when accessed holds a power all of its own.

The Archetype of the Activist

As already explored, therefore, activism is actually a process as guided by the unconscious and manifested by a contained, more porous, egoic sense of self. This movement though is not without risk and danger as there is sometimes an addictive quality to being an egoically or trauma driven activist; that narcissistic belief that one is constantly doing the good that God has sent before us often belies the reality that what one is also doing is marginalising other groups as we blunder our way through a cultural, racialised or genderised China shop. Accessing this within or, as I call it in the title of this particular section, the archetype of the activist, is actually a more reflective and in many ways a more painful path for the activist to take, acknowledge, and manifest.

To explore what I mean by the archetype of the activist, it is worth revisiting some of the work of Carl Jung and his ideas about archetypes (C. G. Jung, 1972). Archetypes simplistically put are patterns of creation. There are certain behaviours and actions which are universal and are often told and explored through the symbolism and the metaphors of the varying cultures and societies of planet earth. That these symbols, these behaviours, that these stories are recurrent themes across the planet was an idea that Jung brought to prominence within Western psychology. His idea was that the universality of these myths and metaphors meant that there were certain ideas, feelings, sensations, behaviours, and ways of being which were universal and therefore archetypal. The activist is one of those. Yet to access this part does not just occur because one has been called to do it based upon one's trauma, but one is kept on that path in order to discover an inner vocation built around the idea of change.

Vocation in this instance is an idea put forward by James Hillman (1996) in his work around individuation. As previously stated, individuation involves the separation in these instances from the socially constructed aspects of one's identity. The individuation in this instance also involves the recognition and the acknowledgement of, and separation from, the internalised supremacist which sits within each and every one of us. It should be said, though, there is often a period of suffering that goes within this process of change and development, and that this movement from an inauthentic egoically focused trauma driven activism to one which is more morally driven is a particularly challenging one.

To borrow from the story of Nelson Mandela is a permanent example of this (Mandela, 1994). His activism began from an early age it appears and he was very much focused upon an ideal whereby he foresaw the liberation of South Africa; a South Africa which at the time was under the minority white rule, a rule implemented during the time of colonialism. Some of Mandela's earlier actions in the fight for equal rights, actually involved some quite violent acts. His actions were no different to many other activists of the day across the world, the fight to be recognised and seen, actions it was felt would only be respected if done by force. These actions then of course led to Mandela being incarcerated at Robin Island.

It was during this period of time though where, in many ways, although the light that flame of internal truth still flamed brightly within him, the period of introspection and reflection in his own words changed Mandela from the man he was, a young activist, fighter, to a man of wisdom and greatness who was released from jail so many years later and subsequently led his country to its freedom from the horrors of apartheid (Mandela, 1994).

This simplistic version of a far longer story is not just limited to a man fighting against one of the structures of white supremacy. This inner calling, the inner activist, was also there in Sylvia Pankhurst who I discussed earlier in this book. She took that fire, that drive, harnessed it, reflected upon it during the times when she was incarcerated in prison under the cat and mouse laws of the time, and used it to benefit others still. There are many others who have taken this persistent drive to achieve the rights that their particular group deserves.

Peter Tatchell is another who to date in the writing of this book has been arrested some 100 times and suffered 300 violent assaults by homophobes and far right extremists, including 50 attacks on his flat. Yet, through his work, he has never stopped fighting and advocating for the rights of the LGBTQ community. These are not people who seek out the limelight, these are not people who quest to be seen as a paragon of virtue and upholder of what is right in the world. The egoically driven activist, in their trauma laced activism will, whilst they are already fighting for one form of equality, allow themselves to be co-opted by another one of the structures of supremacy in order to reinforce their message, thereby contradicting the messages that they are trying to express and implant and the changes they are trying to make.

So, whilst the trauma driven activist mobilises the trauma, the anger, the sadness, and the rage of those who have been impacted by other forms of systemic violence, what the morally driven activist does is become a beacon. They sit in the pain of their incarceration; they stay not quite centred within the confinement of their trauma. They live with it instead of acting from within it. They do not so much befriend it as they recognise its pull when it is time for that part, that damaged internalised aspect of one's own inner child, inner person, inner parent, to be held, looked after, contained, nurtured, and loved. In that beacon-ship they bring a sense of hope. Hope here is something that can often be lost for the trauma driven activist. That sense that things will change and yet as my earlier dream suggested, recognising that hope is a constant was something that Job recognised finally in his expressions with God (Carl Gustav Jung, 2002).

Within that beacon-ship, the morally driven activist is also grounded. They recognise that in order for them to do the work that they need to do, to become the extraordinary people that they need to be, there is something within themselves that must be tethered to the ground, be it through family or friends or their own society or culture, something which they can keep for themselves. They have the wisdom, not necessarily the learnedness of reading numerous books in a British library, but the wisdom built out of reflection and reflexivity and understanding and a consideration of their own intersectional identities. Allied to this they also have faith. They have belief that what they are doing right now is for the best, even if it involves a level of self-sacrifice along the way. Like the perfect example of the LGBTQ activist Harvey Milk, reflexivity, hope, and faith are the cornerstones of the morally driven activist (Van Sant, 2008).

Now, this is not some sort of hippy narrative I am trying to express here because this is not the spiritual bypassing of the pain of individuation that is often posited in our transpersonal courses and in our trainings (Walach, 2008). This is the recognition that this process involved both a prolonged period of self-consideration about one's own sense of otherness, together with recognition and containment of the traumatic experiences that have led one to this point as an activist right here, right now. There is an understanding that through an exploration of all of this one might if we are lucky, begin to walk that long, lonely, deep, painful, sensitive, labyrinthine road, a road which is occasionally covered over in brambles that one has to uncover for one's own self to a point where we become a beacon for others.

This next section explores how, in a series of dreams from my own process, this walking towards a decolonising of one's own self and a recognition of one's own sense of freedom can begin. The dreams are not to say that it is over. They are though to say that actually some of these wounds run very deep and unless we explore them, then we run the risk that our activism becomes no less oppressive no less supremacist than any of the structures we are fighting against.

Decolonising the Psyche through Dreams

As previously stated, one of the best routes to understanding the internalised experience of supremacy is through the dreamscape (Johnson, 1986; D. Turner, 2016). It is by accessing the dreams of our clients that we are best positioned to start to recognise how the internalised supremacist dominates the psyche within us all. For this particular section, I am therefore going to be using a number of dreams from my own process to underline and show how not only an understanding of this aspect of all our psyches, but also to sort of look at and consider the aforementioned movement from the trauma driven activism which becomes a start point for all our processes in decolonising or recognising the unconscious supremacist, to one where there is a sense of morally driven activism.

To restate, trauma driven activism, whilst a useful and important touchstone to a deeper sense of morality for us all, in distortion can become complicit in the oppression not just of oneself, but of others around us accordingly. The first dream emphasises this fact fairly well. To offer you a bit of background to these dreams, these were collated during the autumn of 2020, during a period of time when the United Kingdom was under Lockdown over the Christmas period. As previously stated at varying points in this book, the Lockdowns because of COVID-19 have had a disproportionate impact on a good number of minority groups who were either unable to move out of cityscapes and escape to the country, and therefore isolate out in the open air, or had to keep on working and risk their lives because they were on the front lines of the capitalist system we all reside within (Ahrens et al., 2021; Kim & Asbury, 2020).

The first dream though was this one:

> Dream on 20 December 2020. Within this dream I am in a room and there is a white woman trying to stab me in the eye with a pencil. I am fighting for my life in this dream as she aims this pencil at my eye over and over again. Eventually, she stops and goes away. Within this dream, I realise that not only was she trying to blind me, but that she was also trying to kill me.

One of the most important things to recognise about this dream is that the internalised supremacist has taken on the form of the racialised and genderised other, in this case a white woman. The attempt to destroy who I am, to take away that part of myself which marks me out as different, is an aspect of the colonisation of the self, whereby in order to fit in within a cultural narrative one has to kill off or destroy that which marks oneself out as different (D. D. L. Turner, 2021).

It should be noted that one of the other important things about this particular dream is that for many men of colour the most frightening person in a white environment is not actually white men, it is often middle class, often heterosexual white women. The perfect example of this, as mentioned previously in this book, is the Amy Cooper incident in Central Park in the days before George Floyd's murder (Unknown, 2021). As previously stated, the fact that this woman was able to make a false allegation about a man of colour in its Karenesque way, emphasises the power of the internalised supremacist within white, heterosexual femininity. As discussed earlier, the misuse of that power to co-opt or to re-adhere to a patriarchal narrative, then leads to the oppression of the racialised other by white men on behalf of white women. Such as in films such as Birth of a Nation (Griffiths, 1915) whereby patriarchal narratives and racialised narratives are combined intersectionally to provide a web whereby the oppressions of the racialised other can continue. What also has to be acknowledged is that even with the strength of the feminist narrative against the patriarchy, for plenty of others, and this does not just include women, the patriarchy provides a layer of safety against the racialised other, much like it will do against the less abled, the class other and those of different sexuality.

Decolonisation within the dreamscape here involves the recognition of that which has become internalised from engagement within majority environments. This could be for persons from the LGBTQ community the recognition that there will be an internalised homophobe that hates their own sexuality, something internalised from their own family, culture, and political structure. Another example, this could also involve a recognition of the internalised patriarch for those women who find it hard to find their voice in male orientated environments. Or this could involve recognising the internalised ableist whose language and demeanour leads to the repression and suppression of a client's neurodiversity. These symbols will reside in the unconscious space of each of us. We are all supremacists, and this is why the system maintains its power over us all.

The second dream is important though as we start to explore this to a far deeper level.

Dream on 25 December 2020. Within this dream, I am four different types of dogs at four different types of dog show in southern Ireland. The first two dog shows were held in the morning and the last two are in the evening or are now. I am waiting patiently at each one of these dog shows for a white woman to come and judge me as being worthy or not of a prize. The dream ends with me sitting compliantly waiting for this assessment to be made.

This dream actually begins by speaking about the transgenerational nature of the internalised oppression and supremacism. Some of those reading this will recognise the link between the Irish and the Caribbean experience of coming to a country like the United Kingdom during the Windrush years. During this period, often hotels and lodgings had up signs in their windows stating no Blacks, no Irish, no dogs and the more right-wing governments of the time often ran on anti-immigrant policies aimed at the former colonies (Oliver-Dee, 2017). In my twenties, I remember working in environments whereby the Irish and the West Africans were seen as the biggest perpetrators of fraud in this country, where great steps were taken to deny and exclude often on the basis of stereotypes and innuendo and not always on the truth. This dream emphasises that and speaks to some of the unconscious internalisation apparent within it.

The other part, the waiting for the white woman who is going to be judging us, speaks of the supremacist who has got ultimate power to define who I am within the dream. Anything instinctual is placid and compliant and waiting out of fear of not being seen as good enough. It is a slightly different dream from the first one where anything different is destroyed. In this case, there is a kind of acculturated status quo whereby anything that one might happen to be is not seen as too threatening and in need of destruction (Finch & Vega, 2003; Howarth et al., 2014). The third dream though actually speaks of something transforming and changing in those moments.

Dream on 28 December 2020. I am at a spa, and I am in a pool with several beagle dogs and a white woman, and we are all playing and swimming in this space. As we swim and play, a friend of mine, Erin and her partner actually join us in the pool and start to swim with us. My friend, Erin states that she is glad that she is there because she had some time off and wanted to join us. As we play, I look to my right, and I see in an alcove to the pool that there are several white, late teenage girls who are all being mean to each other. As they talk and bicker and banter, one pushes another girl into their part of the pool. I turn back to where I am with my friends and the beagle dogs, and we continue to play amongst ourselves.

The importance of this dream should not be understated in comparison to the other before it. Whereas with the previous dreams, there is even an attempt at the destruction of that more instinctual side of myself or of that which marked me out as the other, in this particular dream the instinctual is free to play and to just be. The need to conform, the awaiting for assessment and judgement is no longer there. It has changed into something more genuine, and authentic in many ways.

The other part to recognise in this dream is that the internalisation of the supremacist, which in this form has come up as a white woman has not gone, but it is contained to its own part of the pool where it will play out its own destructive nature accordingly. Decolonisation of the psyche does not just involve ridding oneself of what had become internalised. For me, in my research, decolonisation of the psyche is actually about recognising what is there and learning to listen to more than just that part of ourselves. Instead of splitting oneself in two and conforming with the internalised coloniser, or the internalised homophobe, or the internalised patriarch, what one needs to be able to do is to listen to it and recognise that it is not always, or even very often, right.

The last part of this particular exploration that I want to acknowledge is the fact that within this dream there is a character here which represents the transgenerational nature of transformation. In my own therapy, one of the most important things that I realised, and I have discovered through working with my therapist, is that the word 'Erin' is actually Gallic for Irish. The transgenerational wound which sat within me had also been changed accordingly.

When doing this sort of exploration, it is important to recognise that the symbols, although internalised, are used not to state that one hates that which might be seen as external but to recognise that actually, we have all imbibed unconsciously the structures of supremacy which makes us conform to certain criticised ways of being. To talk to these and to explore these takes us a massive step forward as we start to recognise and see who we are without them. Subsequent dreams and subsequent experiences have actually been more about discovering who I am as a man, as a black man, and more importantly as an activist, not that I am without and totally devoid of those structures, but in a way that means that I am challenging and working through those internalisations within the Activist Psychotherapist that is Dr Dwight Turner.

Summary

This chapter has worked incredibly hard to show a few different things. Firstly, psychotherapy has a lot of material to offer from its extensive annals of knowledge in the understanding of the internalised political structures by which we are all moulded. Recognising that as well as us having to split and repress aspects of who we are in order to conform to ways of being as given to us by our family, we use the same defences in order to adapt to the political landscapes which circle around us at all times. Be these landscapes patriarchal, white supremacist, or capitalist, they will have impact on all of us here in the global north because this is the environment, the systemic environment, which we have all been raised within.

The second part is to recognise that there is a big difference between activism which is driven by one's own unresolved trauma and activism which is driven by an internal unconscious need to do the right thing today. One is more about the idea that only on one's own will one save others from suffering. That very narrow perspective on the archetype of the hero and the rescuer is posed in my section in the archetype of the activist. This movement though, from that position to a place where one is more morally driven, ultimately involves a lot of pain and a lot of self-reflection. Being an activist is not an easy process and may often involve either the sacrificing of one's own life, one's own being, or the sacrificing of other relationships with other people and the ostracisation of one's own self as one quests for an idea.

There are numerous examples from popular culture and from the classics of those who have undertaken these types of journeys and have found themselves as a consequence of said journey whilst doing incredible things, from Homer's The Odyssey to Frank Miller's Born Again (1987, 2016), the Marvel Graphic Novel where Daredevil, aka Matt Murdock, enters a descent into a personal hell at the hands of the Kingpin. Stories abound of archetypal heroes who have struggled and fought for the other and have been transformed as a part of that whole process.

The next part is the recognition and the exploration through not just this chapter but through previous chapters as well that these internalisations can be recognised, seen, and explored through using creative techniques such as sand play and such as working with one's dreams. Carl Jung for all his flaws was right about the idea that the shadow can be knowing through dreams that our darker impulses are there in the unconscious waiting to be re-discovered. The aspects of my personal dreams of being my own white supremacist, although a facet of being raised within a culture alien to my own, and also being passed down to me trans-generationally, show that I too have aspects of this part of myself which needed to be held and contained and managed.

The reality is therefore that whilst I do not believe that I or any other activist is perfect, what I do believe is that those that I feel safest with are those who have ventured beyond their own trauma in order to explore and understand that which has motivated them to become the wounded healers, nee wounded activist healers, that they are today.

Lastly, psychotherapy, psychology, psychiatry, and all the helping professionals, be they social workers or otherwise, have a duty to recognise that actually their clients, the people they are working with, whilst psychologically driven into their malaise, may also be politically driven to said psychological distraction. This is not to say that as professionals within the health professions, we might be able to alleviate those politically constructed ailments for our clients, but it is to say that our awareness of them brings a greater understanding of just how impacted our clients, our patients and those under our care truly are within the current systems they reside within.

A couple of final points about this though. It is important to recognise that our intersectional identities are malleable and accordingly our external political positions may vary from practitioner to practitioner. I am not particularly an advocate for a singular line of being when it comes to our political standpoint. I am rather more an advocate for healthy or otherwise discussion and ownership of whatever that political position happens to be. As previously explored, the political left in their adherence to the idea that if one holds certain political views that one needs to be silenced, has done not much more psychologically than to create a collective shadow around that silenced perspective. This toing and froing, yinging and yanging, of ideals and perspectives leaves doorways open for political parties to therefore take upon themselves the role of advocate for those disadvantaged and silenced individuals and groups.

A healthy society can therefore hold those tensional opposites. It can sit with the discomfort of hearing where that other person is coming from. It can be a person of colour listening to Steve Bannon's latest discussions in the Oxford Union. It can be feminists who have sat with clients who claim to be from the Incel groups. That challenge does not change our position necessarily, but it does allow for a tension of opposites to build between subject and other, self, and other in a way that often groups, especially within the political arena do not advocate for.

The dreams speak in some way to that. There is no destruction of the supremacist part. It is still there at the side of the pool towards the end. In fact, what is also there is the ally. When we are driven by our trauma then there is an attempt to silence and rid oneself of that other, thereby re-creating the cycle of self-destruction. But, only by recognising that and holding that other, in one's own mind having that projection return home, can there ever really be political peace, capital growth, and psychological prosperity.

This book will be remiss though without some kind of exploration of a final group or other. The planet has suffered as much as any other group in its othering by supremacist forces. That this climate emergency that we are all walking through has a psychological component which is often something which gets missed within mainstream psychotherapy strangely. In a way, similar to just how the pandemic of COVID-19 impacted client and therapist alike, it would therefore seem strange for this part of our global emergency to be left outside of the psychotherapy room and whilst there are a growing number of tests and research papers being written and constructed around the psychological impact of the climate emergency, the last chapter for this book will involve an exploration of just how othered our planet has become in relation to supremacies triumvirate.

References

Adey, P. (2020). *The Handbook of Displacement*. Palgrave.

Ahrens, K. F., Neumann, R. J., Kollmann, B., Plichta, M. M., Lieb, K., Tüscher, O., & Reif, A. (2021). Differential impact of COVID-related lockdown on mental health in Germany. *World Psychiatry*, *20*(1), 140–141. 10.1002/wps.20830

Akbar, N. (1984). *Breaking the Chains of Psychological Slavery*. New Mind.

Alyukov, M. (2022). Making sense of the news in an authoritarian regime: Russian television viewers' reception of the Russia–Ukraine conflict. *Europe - Asia Studies*, *74*(3), 337–359. 10.1080/09668136.2021.2016633

Bachmann, C. L., & Gooch, B. (2017). *LGBT in Britain: Hate Crime and Discrimination*. https://www.stonewall.org.uk/lgbt-britain-hate-crime-and-discrimination

Beevor, A. (1999). *Stalingrad*. Penguin Books Limited.

Benjamin, J. (1998). *Shadow of the Other*. Routledge.

Bookman, M., & Aboulafia, M. (2000). Ethics of care revisited: Gilligan and Levinas. *Philosophy Today*, *44*(9999), 169–174. 10.5840/philtoday200044supplement19

Butler, J. (1997). *The Psychic Life of Power*. Stanford University Press.

Campbell, J. (2021). *Talking at the Gates: A Life of James Baldwin*. Polygon.

Coates, M. (2014). *Denazifying Germany: German Protestantism and the Response to Denazification in the American Zone, 1945–1948* (Issue September). University of York.

Enver, S. (2022, June). It took a human rights court to halt No 10's Rwanda flight – and act with basic humanity. *Guardian Online*, *10*, 1–3. file:///C:/Users/dturn/OneDrive/PhD Folder/Extra articles/ProQuestDocuments-2022-07-13.pdf

Finch, B. K., & Vega, W. a. (2003). Acculturation stress, social support, and self-rated health among Latinos in California. *Journal of Immigrant Health*, *5*(3), 109–117. 10.1023/A:1023987717921

Freud, S. (2014). *On Narcissism*. Penguin Limited.

Gilligan, C. (2014). Moral injury and the ethic of care: reframing the conversation about differences. *Journal of Social Philosophy*, *45*(1), 89–106. 10.1111/josp.12050

Griffiths, D. W. (1915). *Birth of a Nation*. Epoch Producing Co.

Haukkala, H. (2015). From cooperative to contested Europe? The conflict in Ukraine as a culmination of a long-term crisis in EU–Russia relations. *Journal of Contemporary European Studies*, *23*(1), 25–40. 10.1080/14782804.2014.1001822

Held, V. (2014). The ethics of care as normative guidance: comment on Gilligan. *Journal of Social Philosophy*, *45*(1), 107–115. 10.1111/josp.12051

Hillman, J. (1996). *The Souls Code: In Search of Character and Calling*. Ballantine Books Inc.

Homer, S. (2007). *Jacques Lacan: Routledge Critical Thinkers (Kindle Edition)*. Routledge.

Homer, S. (2016). *The Odyssey*. Digireads.com Publishing.

Howarth, C., Wagner, W., Magnusson, N., & Sammut, G. (2014). 'It's only other people who make me feel Black': acculturation, identity, and agency in a multicultural community. *Political Psychology*, *35*(1), 81–95. 10.1111/pops.12020

Johnson, R. A. (1986). *Inner Work: Using Dreams and Active Imagination for Personal Growth*. Harper San Francisco.

Jung, C. G. (1972). *Four Archetypes*. Routledge.

Jung, C. G. (2002). *Answer to Job* (2nd ed.). Routledge.

Kim, L. E., & Asbury, K. (2020). 'Like a rug had been pulled from under you': the impact of COVID-19 on teachers in England during the first six weeks of the UK lockdown. *British Journal of Educational Psychology*, *90*(4), 1062–1083. 10.1111/bjep.12381

Kristeva, J. (1994). *Strangers to Ourselves*. Columbia University Press.

Lacan, J. (2003). *The Cambridge Companion to Lacan* (J.-M. Rabate (ed.)). Cambridge University Press. 10.1017/CCOL0521807441

Luna, A. M. (2015). The components of dehumanization. *Peace and Conflict Studies*, *22*(1), 18–33.

Mandela, N. (1994). *Long Walk To Freedom*. Abacus Publishing.

Miller, F., & Mazzucchelli, D. (1987). *Daredevil: Born Again*. Marvel Entertainment Group Limited.

Mitchell, J. (1986). *The Selected Melanie Klein*. Penguin Limited.

Oliver-Dee, S. (2017). Integration, assimilation and fundamental British values. *Cambridge Papers*, *26*(3), 1–6.

Perry, J. C., & Bond, M. (2017). Addressing defenses in psychotherapy to improve adaptation. *Psychoanalytic Inquiry*, *37*(3), 153–166. 10.1080/07351690.2017.1285185

Proctor, G. (2010). Boundaries or mutuality in therapy: is mutuality really possible or is therapy doomed from the start? *Psychotherapy and Politics International*, *8*(1), 44–58. 10.1002/ppi

Rouholamin, C. (2007). The 'frame' as a container for the erotic transference – A case study. *Psychodynamic Practice*, *13*(2), 167–182. 10.1080/14753630701273082

Stein, M. (2005). Individuation: inner work. *Journal of Jungian Theory and Practice*, *7*(2), 1–13.

Turner, D. (2016). Born again: an alchemical exploration of the dreams of the other. *IASD*, *45*, 1–8.

Turner, D. D. L. (2021). *Intersections of Privilege and Otherness in Counselling and Psychotherapy* (1st ed.). Routledge.

Turner, D. D. L. (2022). From the Editorial Board. *Therapy Today*, *May*, 2022.

Unknown (2016). *Isle of Man Exhibition Features History of WW2 Internment Camp*. BBC News. https://www.bbc.co.uk/news/world-europe-isle-of-man-36906504

Unknown (2021). *Central Park: Amy Cooper has Criminal Case Against Her Dismissed*. BBC News Online. https://www.bbc.co.uk/news/world-us-canada-56089809

Vaillant, G. E. (1994). Ego mechanisms of defense and personality psychopathology. *Journal of Abnormal Psychology*, *103*(1), 44–50. http://www.ncbi.nlm.nih.gov/pubmed/8040479

Valdés Miyares, J. R. (2017). On the trail of the highland clearances: the clearances metanarrative in Scottish historical fiction. *English Studies*, *98*(6), 585–597. 10.1080/0013838X.2017.1322384

van der Kolk, B. (2015). *The Body Keeps The Score: Mind, Brain and Body in the Transformation of Trauma* (1st ed.). Penguin Books Limited.

Van Sant, G. (2008). *Milk* (p. 1). Focus Features. http://www.imdb.com/title/tt1013753/companycredits?ref_=ttfc_ql_5

von Franz, M.-L. (1980). *Projection and Re-Collection in Jungian Psychology*. Open Court Publications.

Walach, H. (2008). Narciassism – the shadow of transpersonal psychology. *Transpersonal Psychological Review*, *12*(2), 47–59.

Westad, O. A. (2018). *The Cold War: A World History*. Penguin Books Limited.

Chapter 6

The Climate and Supremacy

In closing out this volume of this book on one of the biggest challenges for our age, I think it is appropriate to open with the following quote from the COP26 Conference held in 2022 in Glasgow:

> In December 2015, agreement was reached at COP21 in Paris to keep a global temperature rise this century well below 2°C above pre-industrial levels and to pursue efforts to limit the temperature increase even further to 1.5°C. The Paris Agreement entered into force on 4 November 2016 and 191 Parties have ratified the agreement.
>
> (Ares, 2021, p. 5)

According to the Intergovernmental Panel on Climate Change (IPCC), climate change is real and it is humans who have led us to this point (IPCC, 2021). Climate change involving the build-up of greenhouse gases in our atmosphere has been scientifically proven to be linked to increased temperatures across the planet. With the biggest amount of greenhouse gasses, carbon dioxide, being produced through the burning of fossil fuels predominantly in countries populated within the Global North.

The link between the increased levels of greenhouse gasses and in- dustrialisation, as mentioned in the simple early quote above, ties Capitalism, and in other ways Socialism as well, to the destruction of the planet we are all bearing witness to. Yet, whilst we walk towards a self-genocidal crisis of unimaginable size, it appears as if governments across the world have in many ways struggled or rejected calls to reduce the amount of fossil fuels being mined or burnt by their cars, their factories, their power stations, etc. In fact, in the recent COP26 conference, out of the many diverse areas of con- cern, the report produced emphasised that the world's struggles to meet sustainability levels by the year 2030 has had a direct impact upon the mental health of many people within these countries.

Given that many of us have watched scenes of fires across Australia, America, and Russia prompted by increased temperatures in certain areas or the release of methane into the air because of the reduction of polar ice caps,

DOI: 10.4324/9781003313229-6

these images have of course provoked consternation and worry amongst our populaces. Tie this together with often rising sea levels in developing countries, or increased temperature levels in sub-Saharan countries thereby making both environments pretty much unliveable, the coming global climate migration to areas of the world where there is food, shelter, and safety, is another concern (Attenborough, 2021).

A recent survey published in *Frontiers in Psychiatry*, provided a link between the observance of the ravages of climate change and the impact upon the mental health of those researched (Cianconi et al., 2020). Moving beyond the 24-hour news cycles, the direct impact of the changes in air temperature, sea levels, tornados and wind-borne systems, and the increased levels of deforestation and the expansion of deserts, has had a direct impact upon many who strive to survive in often very serious circumstances. Whilst, for those who have been able to avoid said impacts thus far, because they have the wealth or the privilege of where they live in order that they might do so, the report also recognised that this experience was lessened considerably.

This distancing of the impact of climate change holds echoes of that around war expressed in Chapter 5, where war was seen as being something 'over there' and not something which Europeans have engaged within for centuries themselves (Haukkala, 2015). Yet, as soon as we contrast this to the recent pandemic, where many of those with wealth and the means were able to move their families out of major cities into the countryside to lockdown in relative comfort, whilst those who were less financially able were often stuck in high rises or inner city areas and able to do the same, then we see a pattern of privilege and supremacy emergent (Balhara et al., 2020; Dib et al., 2020; Stein et al., 2020).

It is not a great leap to suggest that as the climate emergency crawls ever closer to the Global North, those who have the cash and the ability to move themselves will be able to buy their ticket to survive the coming catastrophe. That this catastrophe is very much driven by the efforts of capitalism should not be ignored. Capitalism predominantly, but in no less of a relationship with patriarchal white supremacy, has a particular vision of the planet and the environment, a vision that excludes and objectifies not just the human other but also the animal and the planet itself.

This closing chapter will therefore briefly consider both the detrimental impact of this type of '*climate othering*' as I shall call it, together with the greenwashing that occurs in the name of helping the environment. Actions which are not much more than an attempt by major corporations to maintain their position of prominence and achieve the levels of profits that their organisations and shareholders feel they are entitled to (Delmas & Burbano, 2011; Markham et al., 2014). In order to do this, though, I think it is important to proffer a client example and then to explore said example through the rest of this chapter.

Client example:

I will be calling this client Bernard. Bernard was a 40-year-old man, a former refugee who settled in the United Kingdom some five years ago, during a difficult period where war had impacted upon his country to the extent that he had to leave, otherwise the government in his home country, should they have found him, would have taken his life.

This was not though the main reason for his leaving his home country. Bernard was living in an area of the country that had been not only ravaged by war, but that had been impacted for a number of generations by not only the impact of the aftershocks of colonialism but had been struck by a good number of natural disasters which had left him repeatedly homeless and unable to establish any income for himself and his family. Following the third such incidence of his livelihood being swept away during a cyclone, Bernard had finally decided, along with his family that he would club together enough money to be able to come to the United Kingdom to find work.

His entry into therapy with myself had followed on from a number of years whereby he had struggled to not only gain entrance to a western nation, but once he had arrived, he had struggled to establish himself and find a decent enough employment and a room in a major city from whence he could work. Bernard's life had been a struggle before, but it was also a struggle now. Coupled with this, the fact that he was often worried for his wife and three children, all girls, who were living with her parents back in their home nation, his worry had led to him having a near breakdown where friends had recommended that he seek out some professional help.

Whilst working with Bernard, one of the things that he kept expressing was his incredulity at the riches paraded before him every day. From those who were able to afford their own car to get to work, to those who would wear fairly nice outfits each different day. For him, Bernard's upset, irritation, and near anger was about the fact that he had come from nothing, still had nothing, and struggled with nothing whilst others around blithely wandered about with near everything in comparison.

The Psychological Selfishness of Supremacy

As fairly obvious by now and as previously discussed, when a group looks to achieve supremacy, it does so from a position of selfishness. Said supremacy is designed by its very nature to maintain a level of safety for said internal group against the threats of the other as perceived by the subject. These threats though are often not real and yet existentially in this instance can be felt at quite a deep level as such. In any experience where we meet difference, be it from when we are at school to when we are older and out in the world, that experience is scary. From the first moment two people who have flirted on Tinder decide to actually meet, the fact that they are both performing, suggests that it is not safe to bring a true sense of who they are to bear before someone they do not know.

Encounters with the unknown involve a protectiveness for us and a defensiveness against the other. This is no different when we encounter the planet we live upon. Our life is always an encounter with difference, with otherness. What we see, how we engage with it is tinged with a sense of fear and wariness about that which we do not know. In many ways, we have constructed environments which defend us against the full impact of that which we do not know. How our food is sourced. For those who are meat eaters, how the animals are killed to provide our sustenance. We are defensive against that because if we truly had to experience what it was like for the other to provide us with what we need, then we would choose to make potentially different choices. Not always, but we would think differently about the world around us. The man, woman, or child who wanders through a supermarket and sees their food nicely packaged on a shelf has no idea of the abattoir or the any experience of just how much this animal endured on its way to our dinner table.

We are often blinded from the other, the environment and the animals that live upon it because for us to fully engage with that means we would have to take a different track. To offer a slightly different more indigenous angle, in some cultures in Africa when they used to hunt animals, they would do so with a sense of reverence towards said animal. This was so much so that when an animal's life was taken every part of the animal was not only used, but prayers and rituals were performed about said animal in order to provide a level of respect for the process that that animal had undergone in its sacrifice for us as human beings. Plenty of cultures across the planet see themselves in relation to the world around them and work from that perspective of not being separate to or above but being in relationship with and therefore alongside. Supremacy does not do that. Supremacy in its selfishness is about the self-sustenance needed in order to maintain its level above the other (Day Dane Kaohelani Silva Amshatar Ololodi Monroe, 2014; Mark & Lyons, 2010).

How can one person, one family, one group therefore dominate another person, another group, another part of the planet? What does it need to maintain its profits or its position of superiority? Supremacy over the environment therefore places the environment as just another other to be dominated. It rejects the moral call from within us as previously discussed and the moral dynamic needed in order to live in relationship with the planet in order to take one's super-egoic drive towards a position of priority. More recent examples of this strange kind of narcissistic superiority emerge, one could suggest, from the drive towards space tourism by certain small pockets of individuals, whilst simultaneously millions across the planet struggle for food, water, and other resources. These things, although often pitched as well-meaning and designed to take humanity to the next level with regards to space exploration, are often as much driven by the egoic, self-serving needs of said individuals as they are by any sort of altruistic perspective per say (Marshall, 2022; Various, 2021).

Supremacy does not necessarily care for equal rights to be passed around the populous of the planet. Supremacy in these instances then looks to escape, quite literally, its responsibility for the planet which gave it birth.

The Climate as the Other

Another area to consider when we look at climate change and the influence upon climate change on the capitalist system becomes apparent when we consider the role of greenwashing and just how widespread this actually in making us believe something which is not truly there. The COP26 meeting in 2022 and the climate emergency report of 2021 both highlighted the fact that countries across the planet were not doing anywhere near enough to stave off the coming ravages of climate change.

Greta Thunberg (2021) in calling out a number of countries, including those in the so called developing world as well as some in the Western world, for doing the bare minimum highlights the fact that what they are engaging within is a form of political greenwashing, whereby certain governments will do the bare minimum to reduce reliance upon fossil fuels and such by the minimum amount by 2030, whilst also under-investing, or in some cases not investing at all, in renewable energies which could be used to fuel said economies.

As previously stated, greenwashing is a more common phenomenon than people like to admit and in fact we can all find ourselves falling into believing that we are doing enough by doing out own small part, the small part dictated to us to recycle certain goods or not to drive to work on certain days of the week. The fact that we will also still fail in many, many other areas is not because we are ignorant of what we need to be doing but is in part because our own supremacist need for security above that of our colleagues and those around us.

A perfect other example of this emerged out of the constant debates during the global COVID-19 pandemic where the issue of freedoms was discussed about whether one should wear or not wear a mask. That this piece of cloth became symbolic of the war of words and the tussle of ideologies from individuals, groups, and communities alike, became symptomatic of the fact that we are not all in this together (PHE, 2020; Woskie & Wenham, 2021). The individualisation of communities, which is a pre-requisite of a capitalist society, in that it is each one for themselves and one's individual rights override the rights of a community ad infinitum. This thereby running counter to the ethics of care ideas posited by theorists such as Gilligan where she argues argue that morality is relational, and I will again add intersectional (Gilligan, 2014).

The problem with this individualistic narrative, when applied to climate change and the othering of the world that we live within, is that it denies the actual rights of the planet herself. In a series of interesting political moves out of South America the idea that the planet itself has rights, has been raised and upheld in a series of landmark decisions. In the same way that minority groups across the planet have fought for their rights, those who have seen and given nature its voice, have seen fit to apply the rules of law adopted and used amongst many nations across the planet to therefore force some countries to look after the environments they are embedded within. Though, whilst it is obvious that the planet has no voice of its own, this major step is a powerful one when it comes to challenging and countering the supremacists' narratives. We have already seen how the marginalisation of minority groups can often involve the silencing and the taking away or the co-opting even of their own voice. When that is applied to nature herself, what we also start to recognise is that this is something that we, especially in the Global North, have bought into in the oppression of the world around us.

A second factor, which is also worthy of note, is emergent out of a number of studies whereby groups have asserted their right to live in an environment which is healthy for them and their families and their communities (Berros, 2021; Kauffman & Martin, 2021). These green earth politics have encouraged, and again in some ways forced, countries with political systems to recognise that the environments within which that we are all living within are often not fit for purpose. This could involve the rights for clean water, or with the right to actually live somewhere where there is clean and accessible air is seen as a basic human right.

For example, here in the United Kingdom Southern Water, one of the premier providers of clean water located in the South East of England, were fined £90 million for their failure to actually uphold a series of directives which have underpinned their licence in the United Kingdom (Neville, 2021). Whilst in Flint, Michigan, in the United States there has been a similar fight for clean water rights since 2014 as around one hundred thousand people have struggled in their fight with the United States' legal system to encourage big business to give them the clean water that they not so much need or deserve, but that is actually their human right (Various, 2014).

Clean air policies also fit into this sort of narrative. The rights that we all have to live in environments whereby we are able to breath clean air, have a space to wander out and not be polluted by which will not lead our children or ourselves becoming asthmatic. The idea that safety from the planet's ravages by our own selves has become a privilege for so many is abhorrent.

How we treat the planet in some ways underlines just how far internalised supremacy has gone; that failure to recognise that our privilege, be it through scientific wisdom or through engineering knowledge, means that we have a duty to use our power, will, knowledge, and skill to look after, not just the world around us, but to benefit those who live upon it. The failure to even do so, or if I put this more succinctly, the rejection of said responsibility in favour of endless unobtainable profit, is nothing more than the capitalist supremacists' ideal ravaging the world around us.

Final Words

This book has been a joy to construct but also a very painful one. There have been stages in its writing and in its research and in the research of the topics emphasised in these pages, where even I have felt the despair of the intersectional systems of supremacy that we all live within. There are many areas that I could have also included within this tome but which I chose not to include at this stage because this book would be far too long and unwieldy and because there are other writers in the fields today, of psychotherapy, psychology, philosophy, and other areas, who are as well, if not better positioned to write about some of those ideas and ideologies as I am myself. The painful aspects of exploring the socially constructed forms of our identities are there on these pages presented through the examples of my clients and myself. I will never say that any of this exploration for any of us is an easy one; shadow work never is. What I do say is that looking at our future, looking at our route to individual and collective individuation, and looking at how we start to recognise, explore, and disassemble the socially constructed aspects of identities when they are ready to be taken down, then allows us to start to reveal who we are and our moral responsibility for ourselves, each other, and the world around us. The work therefore continues, in fact I suspect that it never ends, although I hope that on one day in the long distant future may the triad of patriarchy, white supremacy, and capitalism all collapse, and their disassembled pebbles come rolling down the mountain side from Sisyphus' rock.

References

Ares, E. (2021). COP26: the international climate change conference, Glasgow, UK. *House of Commons Library, October*, 1–21. https://researchbriefings.files.parliament.uk/documents/CBP-8868/CBP-8868.pdf

Attenborough, D. (2021). COP26: Not fear, but hope. *COP26, 1*. https://www.bbc.co.uk/news/av/science-environment-59121615

Balhara, Y. P. S., Singh, S., & Narang, P. (2020). Effect of lockdown following COVID-19 pandemic on alcohol use and help-seeking behavior: observations and insights from a sample of alcohol use disorder patients under treatment from a tertiary care center. *Psychiatry and Clinical Neurosciences, 74*(8), 440–441. 10.1111/pcn.13075

Berros, M. V. (2021). Rights of Nature. *Encyclopedia of Law and Development, January*, 253–255. 10.4337/9781788117975.00072

Cianconi, P., Betrò, S., & Janiri, L. (2020). The impact of climate change on mental health: a systematic descriptive review. *Frontiers in Psychiatry, 11*(March), 1–15. 10.3389/fpsyt.2020.00074

Day Dane Kaohelani Silva Amshatar Ololodi Monroe, D. (2014). The wisdom of indigenous healers. *Creative Nursing, 20*(1). 10.1891/1078-4535.20.1.37

Delmas, M. A., & Burbano, V. C. (2011). The drivers of greenwashing. *California Management Review, 54*(1), 64–87. 10.1525/cmr.2011.54.1.64

Dib, S., Rougeaux, E., Vázquez-Vázquez, A., Wells, J. C. K., & Fewtrell, M. (2020). Maternal mental health and coping during the COVID-19 lockdown in the UK: data from the COVID-19 New Mum Study. *International Journal of Gynecology and Obstetrics, 151*(3), 407–414. 10.1002/ijgo.13397

Gilligan, C. (2014). Moral injury and the ethic of care: reframing the conversation about differences. *Journal of Social Philosophy*, *45*(1), 89–106. 10.1111/josp.12050

Haukkala, H. (2015). From cooperative to contested Europe? The conflict in Ukraine as a culmination of a long-term crisis in EU–Russia relations. *Journal of Contemporary European Studies*, *23*(1), 25–40. 10.1080/14782804.2014.1001822

IPCC (2021). IPCC press release AR6. *Climate Change 2013 - The Physical Science Basis, August 2021*, 1–6.

Kauffman, C. M., & Martin, P. L. (2021). *The Politics of Rights of Nature*. Massachusetts Institute of Technology.

Mark, G. T., & Lyons, A. C. (2010). Maori healers' views on wellbeing: the importance of mind, body, spirit, family and land. *Social Science & Medicine (1982)*, *70*(11), 1756–1764. 10.1016/j.socscimed.2010.02.001

Markham, D., Khare, A., & Beckman, T. (2014). Greenwashing: a proposal to restrict its spread. *Journal of Environmental Assessment Policy and Management*, *16*(4), 1–16. 10.1142/S1464333214500306

Marshall, A. (2022). The public lament of Jeff Bezos' 2021 space jaunts. *PSAKU International Journal of Interdisciplinary Research*, *11*(June), 43–59.

Neville, S. (2021). *Southern Water fined record £90m after admitting criminal sewage dumping*. Independent Online. https://www.independent.co.uk/business/southern-water-fined-record-ps90m-after-admitting-criminal-sewage-dumping-b1881391.html

PHE (2020). *Disparities in the risk and outcomes from COVID-19*.

Stein, H. C., Giordano, B., del Giudice, R., Basi, C., Gambini, O., & D'Agostino, A. (2020). Pre/post comparison study of emergency mental health visits during the COVID-19 lockdown in Lombardy, Italy. *Psychiatry and Clinical Neurosciences*, *74*(11), 605–607. 10.1111/pcn.13126

Unknown (2021). *Greta Thunberg: 'COP26 even watered down the blah, blah, blah'*. BBC News Online. https://www.bbc.co.uk/news/av/uk-scotland-59298344

Various (2014). *Flint Water Crisis Explained: Summary, facts and resolutions*. Water Defense. https://waterdefense.org/flint-water-crisis/

Various (2021). *Amazon's Jeff Bezos reaches space in first crewed flight of rocket New Shepard*. ITV Online. https://www.itv.com/news/2021-07-20/amazon-billionaire-jeff-bezos-excited-ahead-of-blue-origin-flight-to-the-edge-of-space

Woskie, L., & Wenham, C. (2021). Do men and women "lockdown" differently? Examining Panama's covid-19 sex-segregated social distancing policy. *Feminist Economics*, *0*(0),1–18. 10.1080/13545701.2020.1867761

Index

ableism 20, 41, 44, 56–57, 60
Aboud, F. E. 62–63, 86
acolytes 20, 69, 71, 73, 90–91, 119–120
ageism 20, 41, 44, 54
archetypes 130, 139
Attenborough, D. 41, 54, 142, 147

BBC 9, 13–14, 24, 49, 54–57, 59, 88, 113, 139, 147–148
Benjamin, J. 138
Bowlby, J. 11, 13, 61, 75, 86
Buber, M. 58, 95, 104, 113–114

capitalism 2, 7, 9–10, 12, 16–17, 23, 26–28, 30–31, 33–34, 37–38, 42, 44, 52, 85, 103, 112, 126, 141–142, 147
class entitlement 42
class sympathy 46
classism 43–44, 54
climate Change 4, 7, 13, 28, 55–56, 91, 114, 141–142, 145, 147–148
climate othering 142
COVID-19 13, 27, 55, 58, 89, 114, 132, 137, 139, 145, 147–148

decolonisation 117, 133, 135
decolonising 129, 132
Diangelo, R. 25, 47, 55, 70, 86, 93, 113
displacement 90, 119, 124, 138
dreams 11, 13–14, 21, 56, 59, 87, 132, 135–137, 139

ego 10, 26, 35, 48, 64–65, 67, 70, 72–73, 86, 92, 94, 100–102, 114, 118, 139

Fanon, F. 26, 56
fascism 7, 34, 39, 42, 58

Gilligan, C. 138, 148
greenwashing 91, 113, 142, 145, 147–148

Hegel, G. 7, 13, 26, 56
heteronormativity 41–42
himpathy 46–47, 57, 69
historical erasure 49
homophobia 3, 7, 9–10, 20, 34, 42, 44, 63, 83, 102, 111, 125

imposter syndrome 50–51, 54, 60
intersectionality 9, 13–14, 34, 55

Jung, C. G. 12, 21, 121, 130, 136

Lorde, A. 16, 57

male entitlement 42
mansplaining 11, 48, 55
microaggressions 11, 51, 55–56
morally driven activism 132

othering 3, 9, 37, 58, 66, 72–73, 92–93, 114, 122–123, 125, 137, 142, 145

patriarchy 2, 9–10, 12, 16–23, 30, 34, 37, 39, 42–44, 52, 56–57, 69, 73, 77, 83, 85, 103, 112, 126, 128, 133, 147
Piaget, J. 61–63, 88
politics of assimilation 77

racism 1–4, 6–7, 9, 13, 20, 22, 24, 34, 42–43, 47, 54–56, 63, 65, 70, 83, 86, 88, 111, 113, 125
religious supremacism 37–39

sand play 8, 11, 74–75, 103, 105, 107, 136
sexism 3–4, 9, 20, 34, 43, 47, 54, 83,
        102–103, 111, 125
silencing 22, 25, 28, 31, 48, 51, 127, 146
socialism 141
Spivak, G. C. 18, 58
splitting 44, 47, 51, 71, 83, 92, 115,
        118–120, 124, 135
Stuart Hall 25, 58
Super Ego 70
Sylvia Pankhurst 18, 33–34, 40, 57, 131

Thingification 39–41
trauma driven activism 122, 130, 132

white supremacy 2, 4, 6, 9–10, 12, 16–17,
        22–25, 28, 31, 34, 37, 39, 47, 49,
        52, 70, 77, 85, 103, 112, 123, 128,
        131, 142, 147
white sympathy 46–47, 69
whitesplaining 48

For Product Safety Concerns and Information please contact our EU
representative GPSR@taylorandfrancis.com
Taylor & Francis Verlag GmbH, Kaufingerstraße 24, 80331 München, Germany

www.ingramcontent.com/pod-product-compliance
Lightning Source LLC
Chambersburg PA
CBHW050612280326
41932CB00016B/3018

9 7 8 1 0 3 2 3 2 1 7 7 6